Butterflies of the Colorado Front Range

A Photographic Guide to 100 Species

by Janet R. Chu and Stephen R. Jones

Boulder County Nature Association
Boulder, Colorado
2020

First edition published in 2011 as
Butterflies of the Colorado Front Range:
A Photographic Guide to 80 Species.

Second edition published in 2020 as
Butterflies of the Colorado Front Range:
A Photographic Guide to 100 Species.

Edited by Lysa Wegman-French
Design and Layout by George Oetzel and Lysa Wegman-French
Cover design by Jim Primock

Cover Photo:

Viceroy by Stephen Jones

Photo Credits:

John Barr 23, 30, 31, 41, 42, 43, 46a, 46b, 48a, 48b, 49, 51b, 56, 57, 61b, 66, 79, 108, 114, 116; Rich Bray 104; Jim P. Brock 52a, 52b; Janet Chu 24, 25, 34, 39, 44, 55, 61a, 70a, 71a, 71b, 77a, 78b, 81, 83, 86, 95a, 100, 109, 110, 111, 112, 115a, 120; Catherine Cook 85a, 107; Mike Figgs 40; Dan Fosco 54, 63, 64; Eva Getman 37; Richard Holmes 72, 85b; Stephen Jones 22, 27, 28, 29, 35, 38, 39, 45, 51a, 53, 54, 58, 60, 62, 63, 65, 67, 68, 69, 70b, 73, 74, 75a, 75b, 76a, 76b, 77b, 78a, 82a, 87, 90a, 90b, 93, 94, 95b, 96, 97, 98, 99a, 99b, 101, 102, 103, 105, 106, 113, 118a, 118b, 119, 121; Venice Kelly 59, 80a, 80b, 88, 89a, 89b, 92, 115b; Bill May 33, 84a; Lynn and Gene Monroe 26; Christian Nunes 36, 46, 47, 50, 84b; Paul A. Opler 32, 117; Kevin Rutherford title page (Pygmy Blues); Ellen Shannon 50b; Dave Sutherland 91

Back cover photos

Clockwise from upper left: Arrowhead Blue (Stephen Jones), Variegated Fritillary (Stephen Jones), Two-tailed Swallowtail (Stephen Jones), Western Tailed-Blue (Laurie Paulik), Painted Lady (Stephen Jones), Colorado Hairstreak (Jim P. Brock)

About the Authors:

Janet Chu taught high school biology for 38 years and has conducted butterfly population studies on Boulder County open space for 16 years, documenting nearly 140 species. Since 1983 she has organized the annual Fourth of July butterfly count at the Cal-Wood Education Center in Boulder County. As a volunteer, Jan has influenced many bird watchers, naturalists and beginners to observe butterflies and begin gardening with native plants.

Stephen Jones is author of *The Last Prairie: A Sandhills Journal* and co-author of *The Shortgrass Prairie*; *The Peterson Field Guide to the North American Prairie*; and *Wild Boulder County*. He works as a teacher, author and wildlife consultant.

Both authors have encouraged young people to become involved in the outdoors.

Dedication:

To our energetic community, filled with people who are

"turned on" and **"turn out"**

to observe and protect our natural surroundings.

- Jan and Steve

Table of Contents

Acknowledgments

We respect and thank those who have gone before us, publishing more complete butterfly books with photos, including Jim P. Brock, Michael S. Fisher, Jeffrey Glassberg, Kenn Kaufman, Paul A Opler and Robert Michael Pyle.

Ray Stanford has developed and shared comprehensive county maps showing species distribution throughout the western United States. These data have been invaluable to us.

Field assistants spent many hours with us walking the wet meadows and rocky hillsides. John Barr, Amy Chu, Cathy Comstock, Cathy Cook, Larry Crowley, Chris Friedman, Dan Fosco, Janet Hanley, Linda Hardesty, Sue Hirschfeld, Richard Holmes, Asa and Jeremy Hurst, Venice Kelly, Chuck Lowry, Jean Morgan, Pam Piombino and Wynne Whyman provided unending enthusiasm and energy while chasing and observing the butterflies.

Michael Fisher helped with identification of photos. Paul A. Opler, C.P. Gillette Museum of Arthropod Diversity, Colorado State University, has counseled us regarding butterfly identification, name changes, taxonomic order and butterfly-host plant dependencies. Dr. Opler is author of the Peterson *Field Guide to Western Butterflies* and *Field Guide to Eastern Butterflies*.

Larry Crowley and Cathy Cook provided their expertise editing the text for readability and accuracy.

We appreciate the skills of George Oetzel and Lysa Wegman-French in completing layout and editing. Converting the second edition into an e-book was begun by George Oetzel, continued by Lysa Wegman-French and completed by Veronica Yager of YellowStudios. Other members of the Boulder County Nature Association Publications Committee who provided oversight during the process of publication were Sue Cass, Cathy Cook, Karen Swigart, Claudia Van Wie and Howard Witkin.

Reports by Richard Bray (especially alpine observations) and Christian Nunes (especially for Eldorado Mountain) provided data beyond the authors' observations for the Boulder County flight times. Michael Fisher provided descriptive data for butterflies less common in the Boulder area.

We appreciate the sharp eyes and color acuity of Amy Helen Chu and Sharon Daugherty in helping with the photo selection and arrangement. In addition, Amy Chu drew the images in the Butterfly Anatomy section.

Photography is tricky and even though we photographed most of the live butterflies, many of our friends shared their better photos for this book: John Barr, Rich Bray, Jim P. Brock, Catherine Cook, Mike Figgs, Dan Fosco, Eva Getman, Richard Holmes, Venice Kelly, Bill May, Lynn and Gene Monroe, Christian Nunes, Paul A. Opler, Laurie Paulik, Ellen Shannon and Dave Sutherland.

Foreword

When I was growing up in Denver, I lived on the wrong side of the tracks–from the mountains, that is. Mind you, I loved my prairie edges and cottonwood cricks, but I longed for the undulations west of town, where I knew the diversity and abundance of butterflies swelled far beyond my local bunch. Happily, my family often drove to the mountains for fishing or picnics. Maybe it would be Clear Creek Canyon to Echo or Glacier Lake and the ghost towns beyond; or Boulder Canyon up to Nederland and down the Peak-to-Peak to emerge through Turkey Creek, Morrison and Red Rocks. Deer Creek, Coal Creek, the South St. Vrain, the Big Thompson–whatever the canyon, I reveled in those green and rising grassland hills, the serried hogbacks and the first junipers and ponderosas of the foothills before plunging into the deep conifers of the mountains themselves. I knew that the ecotone between mountain and plain (though I didn't yet know the word "ecotone") was a portal into happy hunting grounds for butterflies.

My bible at the time was a maroon buckram-bound volume that I still refer to and consider one of the best butterfly books ever published: F. Martin Brown, Don Eff and Bernard Rotger's *Colorado Butterflies*. What I couldn't find in the field, I found in the pages of Brown. Ridings' Satyrs, Edwards' Fritillaries, Mead's Wood-Nymphs–the names of Colorado's pioneer lepidopterists and the butterflies that bore them drew me toward the storied Front Range and beyond. I came to know the traits of the Rockies' eastern hem that made it special in biological terms: that fecund blend of plants and animals adapted to both higher and lower altitudes, greater and lesser rainfall, with affinities both to the east and westerly. A collecting trip into any Front Range canyon was likely to reward you with surprises, questions and mysteries arising from this bubbling melting pot of butterfly evolution.

Now, here comes *Butterflies of the Colorado Front Range*, just in time to help a new generation of butterfly enthusiasts enjoy and understand what they may encounter here. I wish I would have had this beautiful and brilliant booklet alongside my Brown, to augment its wisdom and take me even deeper into the hills of home. Janet Chu and Stephen Jones have done a remarkable job in selecting the species most likely to be encountered in this seductive in-between land, picturing them with stunning fidelity and introducing us to them through their own deep experience and concise, precise and elegant prose.

For years and years, Jan Chu has been conducting butterfly counts and surveys all over the countryside this book encompasses and all through the habitats on either side, from Cal-Wood to the High Line Canal, Rocky Mountain National Park to Boulder County Open Space. Few lepidopterists have done more for raising awareness and understanding of their local fauna, even adding new species to this well-studied county's checklist. Steve Jones became interested in butterflies at the age of 8, when he chased Lorquin's Admirals and California Sisters through the oak woodlands behind his northern California home. Steve may be better known as a prairie naturalist and regional coordinator for the *Colorado Breeding Bird Atlas*, but he's also documented and photographed more than 60 butterfly species in a single, secluded canyon in the Boulder Mountain Park.

I assure you that these authors and their book will be the best of company as you head out into the Front Range–this magic land where the life of the peaks and prairies meet–in search of some of its most beguiling residents. With its expanded coverage of plains species, the book will serve very well for the High Line Canal and all the trails and open spaces of greater Denver. Whether with net or camera, in earnest or for a day's dalliance, allow these flying flowers to catch your imagination and you won't be sorry. Good butterflying!

Robert Michael Pyle, Ph.D.
Author, *The Audubon Society Field Guide to North American Butterflies, The Butterflies of Cascadia, Butterflies of the Pacific Northwest, Magdalena Mountain* and more.

Preface to the Second Edition

In just eight years since our first edition, cell phones with good lenses have replaced more bulky, expensive cameras, and amateur naturalists are venturing farther into the field to seek butterflies. Butterfly houses have filled with schoolchildren being exposed to the wonders and frailties of these creatures. Citizen scientists have become more active, gathering data relating butterfly abundance to climate change, urbanization and habitat fragmentation. Local butterfly clubs are springing up to observe and photograph butterflies and share field observations. Many friends show us their tattered first edition of our field guide, displaying their hand-scrawled field notes marking when and where their personal discoveries were made.

Awareness of the plight of butterflies has become more widespread. Recent observations indicate that numbers of North American Monarch butterflies may have declined as much as 80 percent during the past 20 years. News media have reported the plight of critically endangered Miami Blue and San Bernardino Blue butterflies, whose breeding habitats have diminished to tiny fractions of their former extent.

Genetic studies have enabled scientists to better understand relationships among butterfly families and species. Thus, researchers have changed some scientific names. Common names have also evolved. We updated scientific and common name in this edition; for these we included in parentheses the names that we used in the first edition.

We and our colleagues have experienced more time in the field. Observations have contributed to the validity of the flight times we identified in both the species descriptions and the Boulder County table. In addition, we obtained photographs that better portray the characteristics of some species. We also expanded the coverage of this guide, including more species in the southern Front Range between Denver and Pueblo. This edition includes 100 species you may be most likely to encounter within the Front Range mountains, foothills and adjacent grasslands.

Introduction

"If this book helps you to see butterflies as necessary elements of an imperiled life matrix–or simply to see butterflies–it will have achieved its purpose."

– Robert Michael Pyle, *Watching Washington Butterflies*

"Which of these blues is that?" our students ask as they flip through the pages of butterfly field guides. They're sometimes overwhelmed by the array of possibilities on just one page. We wrote this book to simplify those choices, focusing on the butterflies to be found along the Colorado Front Range. Nearly everyone loves butterflies, from those who see them flitting through their gardens to others who have read about and marveled over the mysterious migration of Monarchs. Some children raise Painted Ladies in their classrooms and experience their fascinating life cycles first hand. Students have partnered with astronauts who accompany Monarchs and Painted Ladies into space to measure the effect of near-zero gravity on their life cycles.

Biologists have studied butterflies in Rocky Mountain National Park to measure how climate change may contribute to the movement of insects to higher elevations. Since butterflies are relatively easy to observe, scientists throughout the world track their numbers to measure short-term changes in native ecosystems.

We watch butterflies because they're exquisitely beautiful, have magical life cycles and teach us about intricate and life-sustaining relationships among plants, insects and their host ecosystems. We hope this field guide will help you enjoy and get better acquainted with the butterflies of our region.

Geographic Scope

This photographic guide highlights the butterflies frequently found along the Colorado Front Range (from the Continental Divide to the plains) from the Colorado-

Wyoming border south to Pueblo. The Front Range includes Larimer, Boulder, Broomfield, Gilpin, Clear Creek, Jefferson, Denver, Douglas, Park, Teller, El Paso, Fremont and Pueblo counties and encompasses four life zones: plains, foothills, montane and alpine. Though a few of the butterflies treated in this guide are confined to a single life zone or geographic area, many range widely and can be found throughout the Front Range of Colorado.

How this Book is Organized

Butterflies in this guide are listed in approximate taxonomic order by family, genus and species. Each species account includes a photo taken in the field; descriptions of the butterfly's appearance; a comparison with similar-appearing species; habitat; host plants; and life cycle including flight times. The flight times described in the species accounts propose the most likely time for the adults to fly in the Front Range, but these fluctuate and are impacted by a number of variables. Weather conditions can change within and across seasons and years. In addition, the north-south position of the locale (within the over 160-mile length of the Front Range) influences the time of transitions between the seasons.

Besides the identification of general flight times for the region within the species accounts, a table in the appendix graphically describes flight times within Boulder County. This table provides a handy visual guide to butterflies that you can anticipate seeing at specific times of the year. Though based on data for Boulder County, it can be used as a guide for approximate times in the rest of the Front Range.

Encountering new names and terms can be perplexing. A glossary in the back of the book provides definitions of terms used. Butterfly common names, scientific names and taxonomic order vary from one author to the next and even from one region to another. This is also true of host and nectar plant names. Authors often retain common names they learned as young scientists or may even invent new ones. Whenever possible, this guide uses butterfly common names listed by the North American Butterfly Association's

Checklist of North American Butterflies Occurring North of Mexico, Edition 2.3. Common names for plants are from Weber and Wittmann's Colorado Flora: Eastern Slope. For scientific names of butterflies, our main source is Pelham's Catalogue of the Butterflies of the United States and Canada.

For taxonomic order we primarily use Opler and Warren's Scientific Names List for Butterfly Species of North America, North of Mexico. However, sometimes scientific data conflict with what seems logical to the lay butterfly watcher. So when research has separated species that seem to go together to the casual watcher, we have kept those species together. For instance, we have grouped Monarchs and Viceroys together since they look so similar.

Scientific names and taxonomic order change as researchers learn more about the evolution of butterflies and the relationships among families. When a scientific name or common name has changed since our first edition, or when researchers use different names for the same species, we have included the previous or alternate names in parentheses at the beginning of that species account.

Occasionally new research exceeds the limits of the NABA checklist, Pelham, or Opler and Warren, so then we rely on advice from Dr. Paul A. Opler. As the author of dozens of technical articles, Dr. Opler actively follows new research; he is a founding member of the High Country Lepidopterists, contributing member of the Lepidopterists' Society and board member of the North American Butterfly Association.

How to Use This Book to Identify Butterflies

Identifying butterflies can be a bit like piecing together a puzzle. The three main characteristics that contribute to the process are the appearance of the butterfly, the location and the time of the season.

When you see a butterfly, look closely at its colors, patterns and shape. Check the color images in this guide for an individual with similar appearances. Next, see if your location agrees with the habitat description. If you're observing a butterfly in a plains grassland but its favorite habitat is an aspen grove, you're likely not seeing what you first guessed. Third, check the butterfly's life cycle to see if the current month falls within the typical flight times of adults. If the three aspects are in sync, congratulations, you've identified the butterfly.

If these details don't match to your satisfaction, take a photograph if you can, then go to one of the many detailed field guides or websites listed in the references. Though this guide describes 100 of the species you're most likely to find in our area, at least 200 butterfly species have been reported in Boulder County alone. So we strongly recommend you keep a comprehensive field guide on hand, such as Jim P. Brock and Kenn Kaufman's *Butterflies of North America*. In addition, the Colorado Front Range Butterflies website provides excellent photos and descriptions of local butterflies.

Also, make sure you're looking at a butterfly, not a moth. Butterflies fly in the daytime, whereas most moths fly from dusk to dawn. However, there are some day-flying moths. Check an antenna to see if it ends in a knob or hook, which would indicate a butterfly. Moth antennae look like miniature feathers, some as narrow as strings and others wider.

Butterfly Anatomy

Terms used in the book to describe parts of butterfly anatomy are illustrated below and listed in the glossary. To simplify terminology, we use "above" and "below" in our descriptions of the wings. Lepidopterists refer to the upper surface of the wings as dorsal and the lower surface (facing the earth when flying) as ventral.

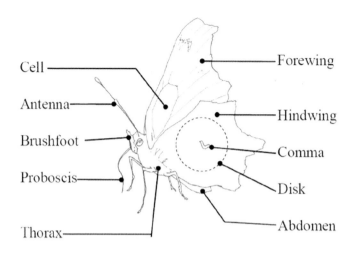

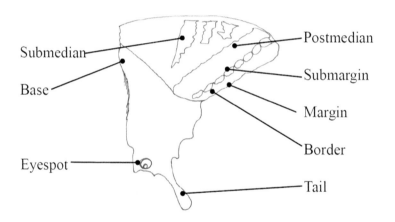

Ecology and Life Cycle

This insect goes through a complete metamorphosis – egg, caterpillar, pupa and adult – to become a butterfly. Caterpillars and butterflies represent two phases of this remarkable life cycle that can be mesmerizing to observe. Butterflies are often found near their caterpillar food, called host plants–the growing leaves and buds upon which the female chooses to lay eggs. She scrapes a leaf with her forelegs and senses the chemicals to know that this is the best plant for her caterpillars to eat. She also uses chemical receptors in her antennae and proboscis. The newly hatched caterpillar often first consumes its own egg shell and then devours leaves, buds or flower petals of the host.

The caterpillar grows and expands its "skin" to its size limit, then out of necessity splits its skin (exoskeleton), emerges with a softened exterior and continues to eat and grow. This molt occurs four or five times; each of these growth stages is called an instar. Finally the caterpillar finds a safe and sheltered spot where it first spins a small patch of silk as an anchor and firmly attaches itself to a leaf, branch or other object. It then sheds its skin the last time, exposing the chrysalis. Within the chrysalis, the contents change form and reassemble; eventually the creature emerges as a fresh adult.

Adult butterflies depend upon sunlight for warmth and fluids for life. Nectar from favorite flowers in gardens and meadows, sap from certain broken branches and even carrion or scat provide sustenance. Butterflies flit over and around blossoms in a great variety of habitats in sunny prairies, rolling hills, steep mountains and windswept tundra.

Most adult butterfly behavior is focused on finding a mate and procreating. Males gather on mud-soaked earth to drink minerals that contribute to the production of spermatophores and their nutrient package. Females fly near the ground, looking for host plants, while males circle over rocky crests and ridgetops, displaying their often magnificent colors and looking for mates. Most adults live for only a few days or weeks, dying shortly after mating and egg laying is completed. However, a few species, including the Mourning Cloak, Milbert's Tortoiseshell and various commas overwinter as adults, surviving for eight months or more.

Adults use a variety of tactics to avoid predation. Some appear leaf-like below, and when hunted by a bird or a lizard open their wings quickly–startling the predator with a flash of color–followed by a quick escape. Some have tails and perch head down. Spots near the tails attract attacking birds, which mistake them for eyes, ripping a beak bite in the wing but missing the head and body. The adult Monarch carries residues of toxins ingested by the caterpillar from host milkweed plants; most birds, after once having tasted this bitter creature, will not attack again.

Monarchs have developed a unique adaptation for avoiding freezing continental temperatures. They migrate during several life cycles, flying from Mexico in early spring to the United States and Canada in summer. The last brood produced at northern latitudes returns to Mexico, completing this true migration. In contrast, most of the butterflies that we see along the Front Range produce a brood here, going through their life cycle once or several times during the warmer seasons, then overwinter as eggs, caterpillars, chrysalises or adults. Some species disperse northward into our area from warmer climes, then die off during winter.

Conservation

Butterflies require life-sustaining environments to flourish and reproduce successfully. Basic to their survival are intact habitats containing healthy populations of host plants. Many habitats along the Front Range are threatened by housing developments, commercial sprawl and roadways. Global climate change poses a very real threat to Colorado butterflies that breed at higher elevations. Within a few decades, warming temperatures may kill the mountaintop host plants of tundra-breeding Bog Fritillaries.

Sprayed herbicides and insecticides challenge butterflies. Broad spraying of pesticides unintentionally poisons caterpillars that eat plants growing near edges of grain and vegetable fields. An insecticidal bacterium, Bt (*Bacillus thuringiensis*), released into the environment to control crop-eating insects, kills nontargeted species, including butterflies.

Fortunately, more and more people are becoming aware of butterflies and working toward their conservation. Butterfly houses invite children and adults to view butterflies close-up and ignite interest in observing their behavior. Gardeners are growing more native plants, understanding that host plants and blossoms will attract butterflies, bees and hummingbirds. Some nurseries specialize in raising and propagating native plants to reduce water usage and increase the availability of nectar. Highway departments plant locally produced seed along interstates. Some parks are leaving ditches and roadsides unmowed.

You can contribute to butterfly conservation by planting native plants in your garden and supporting efforts to conserve native ecosystems near towns and cities. Both the Xerces Society and the North American Butterfly Association websites, listed in the references, provide excellent guidance for conserving butterfly habitat.

Where to Locate Butterflies

Look for areas that have trails into more natural areas. If you find sheltered but sunny water sources, streams, or small ponds there will be butterflies when it's warm. The Horsetooth Reservoir area west of Fort Collins hosts butterflies in its plum thickets and canyons. Around Boulder, Gregory Canyon and Walden Pond are favorite habitats for great varieties of butterflies. In the meadows and woodlands of Boulder Mountain Parks, we've photographed more than 80 butterfly species. High Line Canal in the Denver area provides about 70 miles of maintained banks of undergrowth where swallowtails glide over the long waterway.

The Butterfly Pavilion attracts pollinators like butterflies to an outdoor garden of native plants at its Westminster site (they plan to move to Broomfield in a few years). Within their indoor atrium many subtropical butterflies can easily be observed year around. Denver Botanic Gardens Chatfield Farms provides habitat for hundreds of Colorado butterflies; the enclosed garden in Jefferson County was created in partnership with the Butterfly Pavilion. Roxborough State Park in Douglas County contains the Gambel Oak thickets where the Colorado Hairstreak state insect resides. Lovell Gulch in Pike National Forest near Woodland Park will exhibit many montane butterflies. Lake Pueblo State Park hosts dozens of spring and summer butterfly species in its mature cottonwood groves, streamside willow thickets and rimrock canyons. Many of the state and county parks and open spaces are especially good for butterflies if you can get away from crowded parking lots and overused trails. Search on week days in the many meadows and pathways to find butterflies floating in the breeze.

Watching and Photographing Butterflies

You don't need a butterfly net to enjoy butterflies. Most perching individuals will tolerate an approach within a half-dozen feet, where you can zoom in on them with close-focusing binoculars. With a little stealth and patience, you'll find yourself easing up to within an arm's length of whites, blues, skippers and the occasional fritillary or swallowtail. Photographing butterflies can bring a new dimension to your enjoyment and can also aid in identification of individuals.

Butterflies are most active during clear, calm, warm mornings and afternoons, but if you start looking an hour or two after sunrise you'll have a better chance of getting close. Many species can't fly until the sun has warmed their flight muscles (above about 60°F). During early to midmorning, they may bask on a single perch for several minutes while rousing, giving you more time to observe or photograph.

Birds often attack butterflies, so the insects are vigilant. As a watcher or photographer, try to act as much unlike a bird as possible. Crouch low, approach your subject indirectly and move slowly. If your subject continues to flit away whenever you approach, don't despair. Many male butterflies patrol small territories where they wait for passing females. If you stay with one of these males for a few minutes, moving deliberately, you may get a better view or photograph. The striking profile of the Hoary Comma was taken in this manner. Once this lovely comma accepted our presence, we coaxed it onto an index finger where it imbibed yummy human sweat while we photographed it from every angle. Other butterflies, such as Western Pine Elfins and Taxiles Skippers, return to the same perch time and again, enabling you to set up and wait. Puddling blues may scatter when you approach, but they'll flutter back to their muddy mineral source once you sit quietly or settle down onto the ground.

For viewing equipment, we recommend lightweight 8-power binoculars that focus to 6 feet or closer. A variety of models and brands are available, priced from under $100 to more than $1000.

For photography, a camera with a close-focusing (macro) or telephoto lens will produce the best images. Digital SLRs (single-lens reflex cameras) are particularly desirable, since they give you a clearer view of your subject and easier options for managing depth of field (shallow focus versus deep focus). However, it isn't necessary to have an SLR camera; most "point-and-shoot" digital cameras will enable you to take beautiful photos of butterflies. Some newer cell phones with surprisingly high resolution have telephoto lenses that offer butterfly lovers the chance to get good photos without carrying a lot of equipment.

To improve your chances of getting sharp images, your camera shutter speed should match or exceed in inverse proportion to the length of your focal lens. In other words, if you're using a 200 mm (roughly 4-power) lens, your shutter speed should be 1/200th of a second or faster.

Once you're sure you have a fast enough shutter speed, use the aperture mode of your camera to experiment with shallow versus deep depth of field. Slinking down to the level of your subject will enable you to shoot more artful photos, since you'll be able to "separate" the butterfly (in focus) from the background (pleasingly out of focus). We get some of our best photos while stretched out on the ground. To separate the subject from its background (shallow depth of field), use f-stops lower than f/8. On the other hand, to ensure that the butterfly and background plants are all in focus (a useful technique when you're shooting down on the subject), use f-stops higher than f/11.

That's about it. The key is to get out often, move slowly and be patient until you find a cooperative one. Before you know it you'll have dozens of vibrant photos and, if you're like us, be plotting ways to get even better ones.

Species Accounts and Photographs

Parnassian and Swallowtails

Rocky Mountain Parnassian   *Parnassius smintheus*

Appearance: Snow-white to cream above and below with prominent red and black spots on both forewing and hindwing. Inner wing margins near body dusky gray. Forewing submargin has a dusky gray band. Females display waxy, translucent wings. Antennae have alternate black and white rings. Wingspan 1 3/4 – 2 1/2".

Similar Butterflies: Western White and Checkered White lack red spots and have checkered wing margins above.

Habitat: Meadows, clearings and rocky areas; foothills, montane and alpine.

Parnassians have adapted to life in the tundra, where host stonecrop abounds. Gray scaling on their wings and bodies helps absorb sunlight, enabling them to fly in cold conditions, including snow squalls.

Host Plants: Stonecrop.

Life Cycle: Adults fly late May-early September producing one brood. In alpine environs, caterpillars overwinter in grass clumps or leaf litter; eggs or pupae may also overwinter.

Black Swallowtail   *Papilio polyxenes*

Appearance: Males are black above with prominent yellow spots along the wing edges and a yellow submarginal band. Females are nearly all black above with smaller yellow spots on the forewing margin and prominent blue scaling near the base of the hindwings. Both have long tails, yellow-spotted abdomens and orange, blue and yellow spots below. Wingspan 2 3/4 – 4".

Similar Butterflies: Anise Swallowtail shows more yellow above, in the shape of a solid isosceles triangle. Indra Swallowtail has an all-black abdomen.

Habitat: Meadows and gardens; plains and foothills.

Paper wasps prey on caterpillars, and introduced European paper wasps have taken a toll on Black Swallowtail populations.

Host Plants: Dill, carrot and other parsley family members

Life Cycle: Adults fly April-July producing two or more broods. Caterpillar is striking green with black bands and orange dots. Leaf-like brown or green chrysalis overwinters.

Anise Swallowtail

Papilio zelicaon

Appearance: Forewings mostly black above with a broad yellow central band and flattened yellow spots along the wing edge. Broad yellow areas show below. Red eyespot on hindwing has a centered black pupil. Tails relatively short. Wingspan 2 5/8 – 3 1/2".

Similar Butterflies: Indra and Black Swallowtails typically have less yellow above and a non-centered pupil in red spot near inner edge of hindwings.

Habitat: Meadows, forests, hilltops and gardens; plains, foothills and montane.

These strong flyers gravitate to hilltops where they cruise for mates. A swallowtail chrysalis may dangle for more than one year, delaying emergence until weather conditions are favorable and host plants are succulent.

Host Plants: Parsleys, including dill and fennel.

Life Cycle: One to two Colorado broods. Adults fly March-August. Turquoise-and black-banded, orange-spotted caterpillar feeds on leaves and flowers. Chrysalis overwinters.

Indra Swallowtail
(Short-tailed Swallowtail)

Papilio indra

Appearance: Black above with yellow submarginal and marginal bands, often with blue scaling on the hindwings. This pattern is repeated below. Tails usually short. Abdomen mostly black. Wingspan 2 – 3 3/8".

Similar Butterflies: Black Swallowtail has prominent yellow dots on abdomen. Anise Swallowtail has much more yellow above, in a single large isosceles triangle spreading across wings.

Habitat: Rocky slopes and hilltops; foothills, montane and alpine.

Acrobatic males display around hilltops, where they may "joust" in midair. Males also congregate around damp earth and puddles.

Host Plants: Parsley family.

Life Cycle: Usually one brood, May-August. Gray, tan or olive chrysalis overwinters near ground.

Western Tiger Swallowtail *Papilio rutulus*

Appearance: Large yellow swallowtail with thick black stripes and a single prominent tail on each hindwing. Below continuous yellow marginal band. Wingspan 2 1/2 – 4".

Similar Butterflies: Two-tailed Swallowtail has a second tail on each hindwing and narrow black stripes on wings. Eastern Tiger Swallowtails rarely appear in the Front Range.

Habitat: Streamsides, gardens and woodlands; plains, foothills and montane.

Groups of males gather around puddles in late spring. Patrolling males course over stream corridors, coming into view repeatedly as they fly back and forth.

Host Plants: Cottonwoods, willows, alder, aspen, maples and wild plum.

Life Cycle: Adults fly primarily in April to August, producing one or two broods. Young larvae resemble bird droppings but quickly mature into bright green caterpillars with yellowish "eyespots." Dark brown chrysalis overwinters while dangling from a small protected branch.

Pale Swallowtail *Papilio eurymedon*

Appearance: Creamy white above with thick tiger stripes. Wings pale yellow below with dark bands and black margins. Newly emerged adults may look yellowish. Wingspan 2 1/2 – 3 3/4".

Similar Butterflies: Western Tiger Swallowtail is lemon-yellow above.

Habitat: Hillsides and canyons; plains, foothills and montane.

The buoyant, erratic flight of swallowtails makes them difficult to approach and photograph. However, if a cloud hides the sun, they may linger on a single perch while waiting for the sunlight to warm their flight muscles.

Host Plants: Buckbrush, wild plum and alder.

Life Cycle: Adults fly May-August producing one brood. Feeding caterpillar hides and rests on a silken mat sheltered by curled leaves. Bark-colored chrysalis overwinters.

Two-tailed Swallowtail　　　*Papilio multicaudata*

Appearance: A very large swallowtail with yellow wings, narrow tiger stripes on forewing and a second, less-prominent tail on each hindwing. Wingspan 2 3/4 – 5 1/8".

Similar Butterflies: Western Tiger Swallowtail has a single tail on each hindwing and generally wider black stripes.

Habitat: Canyons, woods and gardens; plains, foothills and montane.

This is our largest butterfly; males are hard to miss as they soar lazily up foothills canyons searching for mates. When nectaring on milkweed, coneflowers or flowering shrubs, individuals will tolerate a stealthy approach.

Host Plants: Chokecherry and other cherries; green ash in towns.

Life Cycle: Adults fly April-August producing one brood. Chrysalis overwinters.

Whites, Orangetip and Sulphurs

Pine White

Neophasia menapia

Appearance: White with prominent black markings on leading edge and tip of forewing above and black wing veins below. Female hindwing below has red edging. Wingspan 1 3/4 – 2".

Similar Butterflies: Checkered White and Western White lack prominent dark marking on leading edge of forewing and dark veins on the hindwing below.

Habitat: Pine forests; foothills and montane.

Host Plants: Ponderosa pine, lodgepole pine and Douglas-fir.

Fairly common during outbreak years and uncommon during others, these striking whites float high among the pines, occasionally descending to nectar on wildflowers.

Life Cycle: Scattered groups fly late July-September, when females lay their eggs in rows on conifer needles. In spring, each surviving egg produces a dark green caterpillar with white stripes. After descending on a silken thread, the fully grown caterpillar forms a green and white chrysalis.

Checkered White

Pontia protodice

Appearance: Mostly white above. Female with prominent gray-black checkering on forewing margin. Male less prominently checkered and usually with 2-3 submarginal spots on forewing. Hindwing below has faint yellow-brown veining, which is heavy in female and faint to missing in male. The more-often encountered form has more checkering above than pictured here. Wingspan 1 1/4 – 2 1/4".

Similar Butterflies: Western White hindwing below usually shows pronounced gray-green veining; male usually has more contiguous black submarginal spots above. Westerns more common in mountain habitats, whereas Checkereds gravitate toward disturbed lowlands. Spring White has prominent yellow veins paralleled by greenish-brown scaling below.

Habitat: Meadows, fields, prairies and suburban gardens; plains, foothills and montane.

Host Plants: Mustards.

Life Cycle: Multiple broods, with adults flying March-August. Chrysalis overwinters.

Western White

Pontia occidentalis

Appearance: White above. Forewing has marginal chevrons lighter than and contrasting with submarginal band of 5-6 gray spots. Hindwing has strong gray-green veining below. Wingspan 1 1/2 – 2 1/8".

Similar Butterflies: Summer Checkered White lacks gray-green veining on hindwing below. Male Checkered White generally has 2-3 submarginal black spots on forewing above.

Habitat: Grasslands, meadows and forest openings; plains, foothills and montane.

Tolerance of cool spring conditions enables these whites to range all the way from southern Colorado and the southern Sierras to northern Alaska.

Host Plants: Native mustards and bee plant.

Life Cycle: Adults fly March-August. Caterpillar is inconspicuous dull green to dark gray. Chrysalis overwinters.

Spring White   *Pontia sisymbrii*

Appearance: Male usually milk white, female cream above with black vein-tip checks near outer forewing margin. Brown-black and yellow scaling parallels veins below, conveying an impression of greenness. Wingspan 1 – 1 3/4".

Similar Butterflies: Western White is larger with greenish veins below. Checkered White lacks prominent venation below.

Habitat: Grassy slopes, canyons and pine forests; plains, foothills and montane.

Among our earliest appearing butterflies, Spring Whites flutter over greening hilltops, ridges and canyon bottoms searching for mates.

Host Plants: Rockcress and other mustards.

Life Cycle: Adults fly April-June. Young caterpillars feed on leaves, while older ones feed on flowers. Inconspicuous dark brown chrysalis overwinters.

Cabbage White

Pieris rapae

Appearance: White above with dark forewing tips and one dark spot (males) or two dark spots (females) on upper forewing. Hindwing below pale yellow, greenish-white or white. Wingspan 1 1/2 – 2".

Similar Butterflies: Checkered White has checkered forewing. Margined White has no spots on the wings, prominent veins on underwings and flies in conifer forests.

Habitat: Cities, gardens, grasslands, croplands and meadows; plains and foothills.

This abundant generalist and introduced garden competitor ranges from central Canada south through the United States and into northern Mexico.

Host Plants: Wild and cultivated mustards, including cabbage, broccoli and watercress.

Life Cycle: Adults fly March-September producing three or more broods. Bright green caterpillar morphs into a green or tan chrysalis. Fall chrysalis overwinters.

Margined White
(Mustard White)

Pieris marginalis

Appearance: Pure white above, though sometimes with one or two black spots in the center of forewing and some black scaling on wingtips. Forewing rounded. Hindwing below pale yellow with light to heavy gray-olive scaling over veins. Wingspan 1 1/4 – 1 7/8".

This mountain-dwelling white is easy to identify in spring when prominent dark veins stand out against its yellowish underwings. These markings are not present in the second brood of summer, when some individuals appear pure white.

Similar Butterflies: Cabbage Whites have one or two prominent black spots on their forewings and less visible venation below.

Habitat: Meadows and open conifer forests; foothills and montane.

Host Plants: Rockcress, watercress and other mustards.

Life Cycle: Adults fly April-August producing two broods. Caterpillars are dark green with a yellow stripe along each side. Chrysalis overwinters.

Large Marble

Euchloe ausonides

Appearance: White above with network of black spots on forewing tip. Extensive yellow-green marbling below. Wingspan 1 1/4 – 1 3/4".

Similar Butterflies: Olympia Marble has sparse marbling below and shading (rather than checkering) of forewing tips above.

Habitat: Stream bottoms and meadows; foothills, montane and alpine.

Large Marbles nectar on the tips of slender tower mustards where artfully camouflaged and predatory crab spiders lie in wait.

Host Plants: Mustards, including tower mustard, tansy mustards and rockcress.

Life Cycle: Adults fly April-August. Female lays eggs singly on unopened flower buds. Caterpillars feed on flowers and fruits. Chrysalis overwinters.

Olympia Marble

Euchloe olympia

Appearance: White above with black bar on forewing cell and black wash on forewing tip. All white antennae. Sparse yellow-green marbling on hindwing below. Forward edge of hindwing has rosy tint. Wingspan 1 1/16 – 1 3/8".

Similar Butterflies: Large Marble has black and white antennae and extensive yellow-green marbling below. In contrast, Olympia Marble has scattered marbling below and no marbling on posterior hindwing tip.

Habitat: Meadows, rocky ridges and ponderosa pine woodlands; plains and foothills.

In early spring these small marbles skitter over grassy ridges, nectaring on pasqueflowers. Males often patrol hilltops, searching and waiting for females.

Host Plants: Rockcress and other mustards.

Life Cycle: Adults fly April-August, producing one brood. Gray caterpillar with yellow and white stripes feeds primarily on buds, flowers and fruits of host plant. Chrysalis overwinters.

Julia Orangetip

Anthocharis julia
(*Anthocharis sara julia*)

Appearance: White above with striking orange and black wingtips. Hindwing below has brown or brownish-green marbling. Wingspan 1 – 1 1/4".

Similar Butterflies: No other whites in our region show orange wingtips.

Habitat: Aspen and pine forests, especially in canyons; foothills and montane.

Males fly quickly and erratically along woodland paths and through forest openings, stopping briefly to rest or nectar. We usually see the first Orangetips of spring flying around patches of blossoming wild plum.

Host Plants: Rockcress.

Life Cycle: Adults fly April-June producing one brood. Caterpillars feed on flower buds and fruits. Chrysalis, which overwinters, resembles a green or brown thorn.

Clouded Sulphur   *Colias philodice*

Appearance: Clear yellow wings above with solid black outer margins on male. Female's black margin displays enclosed yellow spots. Wing fringes pink. Hindwing below has several small dark postmedian spots with a prominent silver spot enclosed in one or two pink rings. Some populations include female "alba forms," which are mostly white with a greenish tint. Wingspan 1 1/2 – 2 1/2".

Similar Butterflies: Orange Sulphur is brighter orange above in spring and deeply yellow with an orange flush in summer. Queen Alexandra's Sulphur is greenish below.

Habitat: Prairies, alfalfa fields and mountain meadows; plains, foothills and montane.

Clouded Sulphurs fly by the dozens above alfalfa fields.

Host Plants: Clovers, alfalfa, milk vetches, golden banner.

Life Cycle: This butterfly flies March-November and produces up to three broods. Some adults emerge from chrysalises during midwinter warm spells, but most begin flying when the host plants are succulent and green.

Orange Sulphur

Colias eurytheme

Appearance: Clear yellow with a bright flush of orange on the trailing edge of the forewing above. Wide black borders on upper side of both wings. From a short distance, female Clouded and Orange Sulphurs can be discriminated from males by the yellow checkered spots within their black borders. Wingspan 1 1/2 – 2 1/8".

Similar Butterflies: Clouded Sulphur is very similar but has no orange blush above on the forewing. Alba (greenish white) forms can be indistinguishable from Clouded Sulphurs.

Habitat: Alfalfa fields, gardens, deserts and meadows; plains, foothills, montane and alpine.

Host Plants: Legumes, including alfalfa, white sweet clover, white clover and vetches.

Life Cycle: The adult flight season is long, April-November, and two broods are likely. Orange Sulphurs can complete their life cycle in areas with long freezing winters, whereas many other spring butterflies appear to disperse northward from warmer areas.

Queen Alexandra's Sulphur   *Colias alexandra*

Appearance: Bright lemon yellow above with black border showing in the male, reduced in the female. Below forewing yellow, hindwing lime to olive green with silvery unrimmed cell spot. Wing fringes light yellow to whitish-green. Wingspan 1 1/2 – 1 7/8″.

Similar Butterflies: Clouded and Orange Sulphurs have faint brown spots on hindwing below near margin and females have spots within black border. These two species usually fly at lower elevations.

Habitat: Meadows, conifer forest clearings and edges; foothills and montane to treeline.

These striking butterflies congregate by the dozens on damp earth following a mountain shower.

Host Plants: Lupines, golden banner and milk vetches.

Life Cycle: Adults fly May-September producing one brood. Caterpillars overwinter in the third instar and go through two additional instars before forming a chrysalis in late May or early June.

Mead's Sulphur   *Colias meadii*

Appearance: Solid yellow-orange with violet sheen and black borders above. Wing fringes pink. Below deep green with small pink-rimmed spot in center of hindwing. Wingspan 1 1/4 – 1 5/8".

Similar Butterflies: Queen Alexandra's Sulphur flies at lower elevations and has yellow or greenish-white wing fringes.

Habitat: Tundra and rocky slopes near treeline; alpine.

This spectacular yellow butterfly brightens high mountain ridges. Its breathtaking orange above and vivid green below always catch our attention.

Host Plants: Clovers, alpine milk vetch and subalpine locoweed.

Life Cycle: Adults fly July-August producing one brood. Caterpillar green with black speckles and hair-like scales. Third instar overwinters and often requires two summers to complete development.

Dainty Sulphur

Nathalis iole

Appearance: Wings yellow above with broad black forewing tips and diffuse black spot and black bars in margins. Yellow below with olive scaling on hindwings adorns this smallest North American sulphur. Wingspan 3/4 – 1 1/8″.

Similar Butterflies: No other sulphur in the Front Range is so noticeably small. Other yellow sulphurs that disperse into our area include Mexican, Sleepy, Dogface and Cloudless.

Habitat: Disturbed areas, grazed dry lands, river corridors, roadsides and railroads; plains, foothills and montane.

Some years we see these tiny yellow butterflies flying low over warm trails, staying just a foot or two ahead of us.

Host Plants: Sneezeweed and garden marigolds.

Life Cycle: Adults fly over six months during warm weather in several broods. The number of broods in the Front Range varies depending on weather conditions, but some years these sulphurs form colonies. They are established residents in the Desert Southwest and follow river courses as they disperse northward from Mexico and southwestern deserts.

Coppers, Elfins and Hairstreaks

Tailed Copper   *Lycaena arota*

Appearance: Both sexes have prominent tails on hindwings. Both are brownish-gray below with black spots just above the tail and a prominent white submarginal band on the hindwing. Male is copper brown above with a slight purplish cast, female bright orange and brown. Wingspan 7/8 – 1 1/4".

Similar Butterflies: No other Colorado copper has prominent tails. Hairstreaks commonly seen in Colorado have less distinctive markings below and obvious hindwing spots.

Habitat: Streams, grasslands, meadows, woodlands and sagebrush; foothills.

They inhabit oak woodlands of the southern Front Range.

Host Plants: Currants and common gooseberry.

Life Cycle: Females lay eggs singly; the eggs hatch the following spring. Caterpillars are green. In summer males perch in open meadows, often near streams, waiting for females to flutter by. Adults fly May through August.

Lustrous Copper   *Lycaena cupreus*

Appearance: Wings above iridescent red or red-orange with a black border and scattered small black dots, especially in female. Below, black spots scatter across orange forewing and gray hindwing with a thin red squiggly line showing along hindwing outer edge. Wingspan 1 – 1 1/4″.

Similar Butterflies: Ruddy Copper lives below treeline where docks and knotweeds grow.

Habitat: Tundra meadows and rock slides; alpine around 11,500 feet.

The flash of red-orange against an old snow field or dark talus leaves us breathless. These coppers don't sit still for a photograph, but spring into the air and fly rapidly to a new perch, rest a moment, then take to the wing again.

Host Plants: Alpine sorrel.

Life Cycle: This dazzling butterfly flies up and down talus slopes June-August depending on timing of the snow melt. Egg overwinters where rocks appear to provide some shelter near the ground.

Bronze Copper

Lycaena hyllus

Appearance: Striking gray-white hindwing and orange forewing below, with a thick orange marginal band on hindwing and small black spots on both forewing and hindwing. Above, female is brown and orange and male is purplish-orange, but both display the prominent orange band on their hindwings. Wingspan 1 1/4 – 1 3/8".

Similar Butterflies: Purplish Copper has narrow orange marginal band on hindwing and is orange-brown on the underside of hindwing.

Habitat: Wet meadows and agricultural areas, often near streams, swamps and rivers; plains and foothills.

These dazzling coppers breed in wet floodplains at the base of the foothills. They often fly in late summer.

Host Plants: Docks and knotweeds.

Life Cycle: Males perch on milkweed leaves and other low growth near host plants to wait for females. Eggs overwinter on host plants. Caterpillar is yellow-green with prominent black stripes and yellow dots.

Ruddy Copper

Lycaena rubidus

Appearance: Male is brilliant red-orange above and female (pictured here) dull gold with some black spots and brown shading. Below, both sexes nearly white to pale yellow. Wingspan 1 1/8 –1 1/4".

Similar Butterflies: Lustrous Copper hindwings are heavily spotted. Blue Copper female has heavy black spots and lacks orange marginal zigzag on hindwing above.

Habitat: Sandy flats and open streambed slopes; montane to 11,000 feet.

We have seen these coppers flying in pairs over gravelly parking lots, with the two sexes appearing strikingly different.

Host Plants: Docks and alpine sorrel.

Life Cycle: Adults fly July-August producing one brood. White eggs are laid singly on host plant where they overwinter.

Blue Copper

Lycaena heteronea

Appearance: Male above is bright sky-blue. Female gray-blue with dark spots and brown shading. On both sexes below the abdomen is whitish and wings nearly white with black spots. Wingspan 1 1/8 – 1 3/4″.

Similar Butterflies: This copper looks like a blue, but it has a white abdomen. Boisduval's Blue has bluish body and pale gray to brownish wings with many dark spots below. Silvery Blue has no submarginal spots below.

Habitat: Canyons, brushy slopes, river flats and plateaus; foothills and montane.

Individuals perch on fences and twigs and do not gather in puddling groups, as blues do. Males are swift flyers and tend to remain airborne for long periods while searching for females.

Host Plants: Wild buckwheats.

Life Cycle: One brood is produced May-August when both sexes visit host flowers. Eggs may overwinter and the chrysalis can enter diapause during a drought.

Purplish Copper   *Lycaena helloides*

Appearance: Male above copper-brown with purplish sheen and scattered black spots. Female orange above with brown shading and brown margins as pictured above. Both dull tan below with scalloped red-orange crescents joined into a submarginal band on hindwings. Wingspan 1 – 1 3/8″.

Similar Butterflies: Dorcas Copper lives at higher elevations in the Rocky Mountains, but only an expert can distinguish them.

Habitat: Weed fields where moisture is constant, seeps and marshes; plains, foothills, montane and alpine.

Males perch on low grass and are fast fliers as they patrol for females. Hardier than their size might suggest, these butterflies persist into autumn.

Host Plants: Docks, sorrels, knotweeds and other buckwheats.

Life Cycle: Adults fly May-September producing several broods. Stubby, green-gray chrysalis covered with short white hairs overwinters.

Moss' Elfin

Callophrys mossii

Appearance: Above the male is gray-brown, the female light brown. Underside is usually reddish brown but variable. Base of the hindwing is darker than the area beyond an irregular pale, lighter, median line. Tailless. Wingspan 3/4 – 1 15/16".

Similar Butterflies: Brown Elfin is noticeably brown and flies later in the season. The Hoary Elfin also flies later and is frosted light gray on the outer edges of both forewing and hindwing.

Habitat: Moist slopes, streamsides and canyons; foothills.

This locally rare species is the first butterfly we search for at the end of winter when snow has mostly melted. Adults visit mud puddles. Males perch on branch tips and fly out to challenge passersby. Females hide inside shrubs, venturing out to nectar on spring beauties and salt-and-pepper blossoms.

Host Plants: Sedums.

Life Cycle: The caterpillar's color varies from orange to yellow to pink, with white chevrons. Adults fly late March to early May in about a 16-foot radius area during their one-week life span. Females lay eggs singly on stonecrops.

Hoary Elfin

Callophrys polios

Appearance: Dusky brown above; dark brown below with white frosting on forewing and hindwing margins. Wings below show a dark, irregular postmedian line and are darker toward the body. Tailless. Wingspan 7/8 – 1".

Similar Butterflies: Brown Elfin lacks the postmedian line below and has a reddish blush, as opposed to frosting, on outer wing margins. Moss' Elfin usually has white on its postmedian line below, highlighting the contrast between its dark inner and lighter outer hindwings.

Habitat: Rocky areas, ridges and forest openings; foothills and montane.

This smallest of Colorado elfins flutters close to host kinnikinnick plants, where males perch to await passing females.

Host Plants: Kinnikinnick.

Life Cycle: Adults fly April-June producing one brood. Females lay eggs singly on kinnikinnick leaf buds or flower stems. Chrysalis overwinters.

Western Pine Elfin

Callophrys eryphon

Appearance: Hindwings below have jagged gray and brown mottling with deeply indented white chevrons. Margins of wings are checkered, appearing scalloped. The upper surface varies from chocolate-brown to warmer orange-brown. Wingspan 7/8 – 1 1/8″.

Similar Butterflies: Hedgerow Hairstreak flies in July and is brown below without mottling. Other elfins are unmarked in the basal wing areas near the body.

Habitat: Pine forests; foothills and lower montane.

Pine Elfins perch on the tips of young pine needles. They flutter up and then return to the same perch, facilitating close observation. Spring sunlight reveals these intricately marked elfins resting among greening leaves along forest trails.

Host Plants: Ponderosa and lodgepole pines.

Life Cycle: Females lay chalk-white eggs April-July. Rich velvet-green caterpillar feeds on tender young pine needles. Brown chrysalis overwinters.

Colorado Hairstreak

Hypaurotis crysalus

Appearance: Black and iridescent purple above with a few orange patches. Underside is grayish with a noticeable black-centered orange spot on hindwing near tail. Hairstreak 'tail' extends from hindwing. Wingspan 1 1/8 – 1 3/8″.

Similar Butterflies: Great Purple Hairstreak is iridescent blue and lives only in Colorado's southwest corner.

Habitat: Gambel oak thickets in canyons, hills and bordering fields; foothills and montane below 9,000 feet.

Males perch on top branch tips and fly upward, circling one another repeatedly. This celebrated butterfly was designated the official Colorado state insect thanks to the advocacy of Aurora's Wheeling Elementary 4th graders and their teacher Melinda Terry.

Host Plants: Gambel oak.

Life Cycle: Eggs are laid on bark. Caterpillars live and feed on leaves. Adults roost and fly above bushes late July-August. Adults feed on tree sap and sweet liquid that exudes from oak insect galls.

Western Green Hairstreak *Callophrys affinis homoperplexa* (Canyon Bramble Hairstreak)

Appearance: Grayish to orange-brown above, sometimes with coppery tints. Tailless. Bright green below with weak or jagged (or nonexistent) white postmedian band of irregular spots or dashes. Wings below have brownish border and are tinted reddish-brown toward the following edge of the forewing. Wingspan 3/4 – 1 1/8".

Similar Butterflies: White-lined Green Hairstreak usually flies earlier in spring and has no orange-brown or coppery scales. Below, it has a prominent white line on wings.

Habitat: Sun-warmed pine forest trails and shrublands; higher plains, foothills and montane.

Males fly on ridges and perch, awaiting females that fly near sulphur-flower blossoms. It's a pleasant surprise to find this greenish butterfly on a warm dirt roadway.

Host Plants: Fendler's buckbrush and sulphur-flower.

Life Cycle: Adults fly April-July producing one brood. Females lay deep green eggs on sulphur-flower. Caterpillar is yellow-green, green, or red with two white lines on its back.

White-lined Green Hairstreak (Sheridan's Hairstreak)

Callophrys sheridanii

Appearance: Below rich green with fairly straight white postmedian line. Above brown with few distinct markings. Wingspan 3/4 – 7/8".

Similar Butterflies: Western Green Hairstreak usually has a weaker and more jagged or nonexistent white postmedian line and copper coloring below.

Habitat: Open hillsides and canyons at mid to high elevations, often near melting snow; foothills, montane.

Host Plants: Buckwheats.

Life Cycle: Adults fly April-early June. In early spring we find these vivid green, white-lined hairstreaks nectaring on rose-pink spring beauties. Both sexes visit flowers, but only males visit puddles and areas of moist ground. Females lay eggs singly on wild buckwheat leaves; caterpillars feed on the leaves, flowers and fruits. Chrysalises overwinter. Territorial males often perch in pine duff or in canyon bottoms.

Juniper Hairstreak
(Siva Juniper Hairstreak)

Callophrys gryneus siva

Appearance: Green below with brick-red on the forewing that is often hidden by the yellow-green hindwing. Both wings below show a white postmedian line hugging an inner darker line. Above, soft grayish to rust-brown. Tails extend from hindwings. Wingspan 1 – 1 1/8".

Similar Butterflies: Thicket Hairstreak is brownish with a black-edged white postmedian line forming a "W" below.

Habitat: Juniper woodlands, windbreaks in hilly or mountainous areas and plantings around houses; foothills.

When we walk near junipers we often bump the branches and flush this small hairstreak into the air, affording us a close view as it lands on a nearby branchlet.

Host Plants: Junipers.

Life Cycle: Adults fly May-June. Females deposit green eggs on the host. The green caterpillar has lumps and bumps resembling scaly juniper needles. Adults nectar on buckwheats and composites.

Thicket Hairstreak

Callophrys spinetorum

Appearance: Below red-brown with prominent white postmedian line forming a "W" in front of tails. Look for a small white cell bar on forewing, below. Steel-gray above. With their contrasting ruddy-brown wings and shimmering white postmedian line, these large forest-dwelling hairstreaks create an unforgettable image. Wingspan 1 – 1 1/4".

Similar Butterflies: Juniper Hairstreaks, found roosting in juniper trees and bushes, have prominent tails, yellow-green hindwings below and brick red on the forewing below.

Habitat: Conifer forest openings; foothills to upper montane.

Host Plants: Dwarf mistletoes growing on pines, junipers and firs.

Life Cycle: Adults fly May-August, producing one or two broods. Males perch in conifers waiting for receptive females or sip nectar from flowers on the forest floor. Females lay eggs singly on dwarf mistletoes. Caterpillars feed on the mistletoe leaves, stems and flowers. Chrysalises overwinter. Though locally uncommon, they sometimes emerge in great numbers.

Coral Hairstreak

Satyrium titus

Appearance: Tailless with red to orange spots on the edge of the wings below. A row of black spots circled with white on the postmedian of both wings below. Above is grayish-brown to brownish and lacking spots. Wingspan 7/8 – 1 5/16".

Similar Butterflies: A reddish-orange spot tops a blue patch in the Striped Hairstreak, which also has parenthesis-like parallel lines on the wing surfaces below.

Habitat: Brushy thickets and overgrown fields; foothills.

Host Plants: Wild plum and chokecherry.

Life Cycle: Adults fly from mid-May to late August. The caterpillar has a pink/rose head and green body. During the day the full-grown caterpillar hides in litter at the base of small saplings of the host plants. The adult emerges from a fuzzy light brown chrysalis in two or three weeks. You may find these delicate hairstreaks busily nectaring on profusions of tiny white buckbrush blossoms protruding above the thorn-like branches.

Banded Hairstreak   *Satyrium calanus*

Appearance: Dark gray below with a post-median band of rectangular spots edged with white. Powder blue tail spot rarely capped with orange, and one of the two tails is significantly longer than the other. Uniform dark brown above. Wingspan 1 – 1 1/4".

Similar Butterflies: Gray Hairstreak is bluish-gray below, with a median band often edged with orange, two long tails and an orange eyespot on the hindwing. Striped Hairstreak has white striping below, three tails and a blue hindwing tail spot capped with orange.

Habitat: Scrub oak woodlands and grasslands; foothills from southern Boulder County to the New Mexico border.

Males perch on Gambel oak leaves. Adults sally out to open meadows to sip nectar from dogbane, common milkweed, sweet clover and yarrow flowers. In early summer they are numerous in the oak woodlands of Roxborough State Park.

Host Plants: Gambel oak and plums.

Life Cycle: Females lay eggs on oak twigs, then the eggs overwinter. Adults fly in June and July.

Striped Hairstreak   *Satyrium liparops*

Appearance: This tailed hairstreak is brownish above. Below, it has median and postmedian rows of widely separated thin white lines. A blue tail spot is capped with red-orange. Wingspan 15/16 – 1 3/16".

Similar Butterflies: Gray Hairstreaks are plain bluish-gray below and can often be found tail up and head down on old flower stalks. Banded Hairstreaks have a postmedian line of dark, white-edged dashes below.

Neither Striped nor Banded Hairstreaks are common in the northern foothills. Banded Hairstreaks can be abundant in Gambel oak woodlands of southern Colorado.

Habitat: Brushy areas and thickets near watercourses; foothills.

Striped Hairstreaks are often found nectaring on buckbrush or dogbane.

Host Plants: Wild plum and chokecherry.

Life Cycle: Caterpillar is dark green with oblique yellow lines on each abdominal segment. Adult flies July-August.

Hedgerow Hairstreak *Satyrium saepium*

Appearance: Purplish-green iridescent sheen reflects from the auburn upper side of the wings when the adult is newly emerged from the chrysalis. A short tail is present. Below, tan to dark red-brown background is crossed by a soft darker jagged line. Wingspan 7/8 –1 1/8".

Similar Butterflies: Hoary Elfin lives on kinnikinnick and is dark brown with a scattering of hoary-gray scales below. Behr's Hairstreak is tailless and orange with black bands on both wings above.

Habitat: Open pine forests and brushy areas; foothills and montane.

Males perch on pine branches in the warming sun, while the females flutter below searching for nectar. During some years these drab hairstreaks appear in large groups, while during others they are difficult to find.

Host Plants: Fendler's buckbrush and sticky-laurel.

Life Cycle: Flies June-August at 7,000 to 8,000 feet. Adults obtain nectar from buckbrush and sulphur-flower. Pale gray-green eggs overwinter on host plants.

Gray Hairstreak   *Strymon melinus*

Appearance: Deep slate gray above with orange spot on hindwing. Below, dove gray with both wings showing somewhat scalloped white midline with thin red-and-black line toward the body. Small orange and blue patches ornament the hindwings near the eye-catching tail. Wingspan 7/8 – 1 1/4".

Similar Butterflies: Other hairstreaks are brown and lack the bright orange hindwing spot above.

Habitat: Meadows, prairies, fields and parks; plains.

Gray Hairstreaks often land head down on last year's stalks of yucca or catnip. They're also found near mint blossoms where they nectar. The red spot near the tails deceives predators, which strike at the tails instead of the head, enabling the butterfly to live another day.

Host Plants: Numerous mints, legumes, mallows and strawberries.

Life Cycle: Adults are present all summer, producing two broods April-August and dispersing over wide areas. Pale green egg becomes a grass-green to translucent-green caterpillar.

Blues

Western Tailed-Blue   *Cupido amyntula*

Appearance: Bright lavender blue above with narrow black margin and a small orange spot near the thinnest of tails. Chalk white with small gray spots below. Wingspan 7/8 – 1 1/8″.

Similar Butterflies: Many blue butterflies resemble this tailed-blue, but it's unique in having an inconspicuous orange spot near the tail.

Habitat: Small meadow openings along trails; foothills and montane.

We find this blue puddling on muddy trails or flying low among green plants. Adults gently swipe their hind wings back and forth and wiggle their tails, drawing predators' attention away from their heads.

Host Plants: Peas, including locoweeds and milk vetches.

Life Cycle: Adults flit among flowering plants April-August. Mature caterpillar overwinters and emerges in early summer to feed on pea family flowers, pods and seeds.

Echo Azure

Celastrina echo sidara
(Celastrina ladon sidara)

Appearance: Male silvery violet-blue above with scattered variable spotting. Female has black band on outer forewing. Below, slate gray with kidney-bean shaped spots aligned neatly from forewing onto the hindwing. Faint chevrons line wing margins. By July, tattered grayish azures have lost spots and colored scales. Wingspan 3/4 – 1 1/4″.

Similar Butterflies: Arrowhead Blue has large white arrowhead in center of the hindwing below and small white arrows along the wing submargin. Hops Azure is pale blue and lives among hops vines.

Habitat: Willows and brushy spruce woodlands; foothills and montane.

This early flying abundant butterfly tolerates cold canyons and high mountains. Males congregate at wet sand.

Host Plants: Waxflower, Fendler's buckbrush and bush-cranberry.

Life Cycle: Flying begins in April in foothills and later at higher elevations. Caterpillars vary from yellow-green to pink. Chrysalis overwinters.

Hops Azure

Celastrina humulus

Appearance: Below white with pattern of small black marks varying from heavily marked to almost immaculate. Male is powdery blue above. Female above has extensive black on outer portions of both forewing and hindwing; may have light iridescent blue blending to white. Wingspan 13/16 – 1 1/16".

Similar Butterflies: Echo Azure is more violet-blue above and flies earlier in the season.

Habitat: Brambles and thickets; foothills. Males can be seen flying low near streams, but females stay more at ground level, nectaring and laying eggs.

Host Plants: Hops and white-flowered lupine (*Lupinus argenteus*). Hops Azures are a rare species in some areas of the Front Range because development in the foothills has destroyed the thorny Hops vines where they live.

Life Cycle: Adults fly in June and early July, laying eggs mostly on Hops vines, although some populations use the white-flowered lupine. Caterpillars vary from yellow-green, green, and blue-green to reddish. Chrysalis overwinters.

Arrowhead Blue

Glaucopsyche piasus

Appearance: Large blue with prominent white arrowhead in center of hindwing below. Row of white arrowheads pointing inward is interspersed with black dots on pale gray to dark brown-gray wings. When wings are open the upper surface is dull deep-blue to violet-blue with brown margins. This blue is easy to identify due to its whitish arrowheads and upright wings when resting. Wingspan 1 – 1 1/4″.

Similar Butterflies: Boisduval's Blue flies at the same time but is paler and more iridescent blue above, with no prominent white markings below.

Habitat: Moist mountain soils; foothills and montane. Assemblages of males gather near moist soil.

Host Plants: Shrubby perennial lupines and other legumes.

Life Cycle: One brood produced when adults fly April-July, early at lower elevations and later at 8,000-10,000 feet. Females lay eggs on lupines, wild peas, vetches and locoweeds. Caterpillar is blue-green to yellow-brown. Brown chrysalis overwinters.

Silvery Blue

Glaucopsyche lygdamus

Appearance: Light silvery-blue above with silvery scales over the veins. Below, a row of black round dots each ringed in white decorates the postmedian area of both grayish-white wings. Place a row of precious old silver coins on the table to admire and you've replicated the Silvery Blue's neat round spots. Wingspan 7/8 – 1 1/4″.

Similar Butterflies: Early spring adults flaunt a silvery sheen on the upper wing surface, in contrast to Echo Azure, which is purple-blue. Boisduval's Blue has a T-bone shaped white spot on hindwing below, along with small scattered spots. Reakirt's Blue is smaller with prominent dark spot on posterior wing margin.

Habitat: Woodlands, brushy streamsides and burned-over riparian areas; plains, foothills, montane and alpine.

Host Plants: Lupines, wild peas, vetches and locoweeds.

Life Cycle: Flies from April in foothills through July at higher elevations. Eggs are laid on legumes. Caterpillar pupates into a brown chrysalis that overwinters.

Rocky Mountain Dotted-Blue   *Euphilotes ancilla*

Appearance: Heavily marked below with many black dots and forewing suffused with smoky gray. Prominent orange submarginal band on the hindwing. Male's wings above are deep blue with medium black border, while female's are brown with an orange blended band of spots on the hindwing. Wingspan 5/8 – 1″.

Similar Butterflies: Lupine Blue has an orange submarginal band often capped with metallic blue-green scintillations. Female Melissa Blue has orange band on both wings above, while male has none.

Habitat: Meadows and sunny slopes; foothills and montane.

Despite their quick and erratic flight, dozens of dotted-blues can be found and easily photographed on sulphur-flowers during nectaring and mating.

Host Plants: Sulphur-flower.

Life Cycle: Flies on high prairie in June, but most common in foothills in May-July with some appearing in the mountains in August. Blue-green eggs are laid when sulphur-flower blooms.

Reakirt's Blue

Echinargus isola

Appearance: Male blue above and female brown with blue toward body. Prominent dark spot on the posterior of hindwing can be seen from a distance. The spot also shows below when wings are closed. Forewing displays row of five round white-ringed black spots. Smallest blue in the foothills. Wingspan 7/8 – 1″.

Similar Butterflies: Flight-worn Echo Azure that has lost its colorful scales or a worn Boisduval's Blue may be somewhat alike. Both are noticeably larger than Reakirt's Blue.

Habitat: Open weedy areas, trails, pastures and fields; plains, foothills and montane.

This tiny blue often rests with wings open. It cannot survive freezing winters during any of its life stages, but during summer adults may produce one brood on pea family plants.

Host Plants: Legumes.

Life Cycle: Flies May-September. Populations disperse north during summer and die out, only to move up from the south again the following year.

Melissa Blue

Plebejus melissa

Appearance: Female has a prominent orange border in gray-brown background on both wings above, thus the alternate name Orange-bordered Blue. Male is blue above with narrow black margin. Below, both have extensive submarginal orange spots on the hindwing flanked by iridescent blue-green scintillations. Wingspan 7/8 – 1 1/4″.

Similar Butterflies: Lupine Blues have orange on hindwings only and iridescent glitter near orange spot bands below.

Habitat: Fields and dry meadows; plains, foothills and montane.

Melissa Blues are found in dry prairies or overgrazed meadows. We're pleased to discover this small butterfly on hot dry days when we can find few others.

Host Plants: Lupines, alfalfa and wild licorice.

Life Cycle: Flies April-August producing two or three broods. Caterpillar is tended by ants that share the sweet "honeydew" it secretes. Overwinters as egg or young caterpillar.

Greenish Blue

Icaricia saepiolus
(Plebejus saepiolus)

Appearance: Blue wings above blend to greenish color toward body in male. Female's orange-brown to brown wings may be bluish toward body with black dots irregularly paired. Both sexes have prominent dark bar on the leading edge of the forewing. Below both show silver-white to gray. Wingspan 1 – 1 1/4".

Similar Butterflies: Boisduval's Blue has white-rimmed black spots on hindwing and solid black spots on the forewing. Wings lack orange. The dark cell bar in the leading edge above of the Greenish Blue's forewing is uncommon in blue butterflies.

Habitat: Aspen groves, bogs, riparian woodlands and moist meadows; foothills, montane and alpine.

Greenish Blues associate with red clover in shady, cooler areas.

Host Plants: Clovers and milk vetches.

Life Cycle: Flies May-August up to 12,000 feet. Caterpillar overwinters half grown.

Boisduval's Blue

Icaricia icarioides
(Plebejus icarioides)

Appearance: Male dull blue to violet-blue above with broad black margins. Female brown to bluish with diffuse black margins. Below, spots vary from irregular black surrounded by small white rings to tiny black centered in white. A giveaway whitish T-bone shape that may display in the center of the hindwing below. Submarginal spots larger on forewings than hindwings. Wingspan 1 – 1 3/8″.

Similar Butterflies: Silvery Blue wings have single row of round black spots below and Greenish Blue wings have a cell bar above.

Habitat: Meadows and grassy hillsides; foothills and montane to 10,000 feet.

Numerous individuals skim the tops of milk vetches and perch on the leaves.

Host Plants: More than 40 lupine species.

Life Cycle: Adults fly May-August laying eggs on tender green leaf tips and producing one brood. Caterpillars grow to 3/8″ then overwinter. The following May they continue to eat and grow before forming a green chrysalis.

Lupine Blue

Icaricia lupini lutzi
(Plebejus lupini lutzi, Plebejus lupini)

Appearance: Male is brilliant shiny silver and purplish-blue above with a broad diffuse border on forewing and broad orange-red spot band around hindwing margin. Female above is slate-brown or bluish with orange band on the hindwing. Metallic blue-green flecks below (seen with binoculars) reflect light on the hindwings near the marginal orange band. Wingspan 3/4 – 1 1/8″.

Similar Butterflies: Melissa Blue male has no orange band on hindwing above and female has orange on both wings above. Both sexes show blue-green metallic flecks below. Dotted-Blues have no scintillated spots.

Habitat: Prairie hilltops, forest openings, canyons and tundra; foothills, montane and alpine.

Host Plants: Wild buckwheats.

Life Cycle: Adults fly June-August from 6,000 to 10,000 feet producing only one brood of gray-green caterpillars.

Monarch and Viceroy

Monarch
Danaus plexippus

Appearance: Cinnamon-orange above with prominent black veins and white dots on bold black wing borders. Pale orange to cinnamon-orange below with black veins. Wingspan 3 – 4 1/2".

Similar Butterflies: Viceroy is smaller and usually has a prominent black band across the hindwings.

Habitat: Prairies and meadows; plains and foothills.

Most fall adults that emerge in eastern Colorado probably migrate to the conifer forests of Mexico, where millions of them winter. Milkweed toxins that they ingest as caterpillars protect them from predation throughout their journey.

Host Plants: Milkweeds.

Life Cycle: As they migrate north from Mexico in spring, they produce successive broods. Monarchs reside in eastern Colorado May-September, producing 1-3 broods. Striking yellow, black and white caterpillar pupates into a jade-green chrysalis flecked with gold.

Viceroy   *Limenitis archippus*

Appearance: Cinnamon-orange above with prominent black veins, a single row of white spots within the bold black wing margin and a black line across hindwings. Pale orange to cinnamon-orange below with similar markings. Wingspan 2 1/4 – 3".

Similar Butterflies: Monarch is larger, has two rows of white spots on the forewing margin and lacks the black line on the hindwing.

Habitat: Marshes and riparian woodlands; plains.

Host Plants: Cottonwoods and aspen.

Life Cycle: Adults fly May-September producing 2-3 broods. Freshly-hatched caterpillars eat their own eggshells then third-instar caterpillars overwinter in a shelter made from a rolled leaf, escaping the attention of foraging birds.

Fritillaries

Variegated Fritillary

Euptoieta claudia

Appearance: Wings above show soft orange-brown irregular blocks outlined in black. Black dots appear between veins of submargins. Below, mottled brown with pale median and marginal patches. Orange toward body. No silver spots. Wingspan 1 3/4 – 2 1/4".

Similar Butterflies: Aphrodite and Edwards' Fritillaries have silvered spots below. Aphrodite is strikingly large and bright orange above while Edwards' displays yellow triangles in wide black border.

Habitat: Open sunny areas and waste fields; plains, foothills and montane.

When Nuttall's violets bloom in April, legions of Variegated Fritillaries often fly low over grasslands and meadows searching for nectar. It's a surprise to see these fritillaries laying eggs on mowed scrubby flax.

Host Plants: Violets and wild flax.

Life Cycle: Adults fly throughout the summer producing one or two broods on the Great Plains. This common subtropical butterfly strays into the Front Range but does not overwinter.

Aphrodite Fritillary

Speyeria aphrodite

Appearance: Large and showy red-orange above with bold black bars and spots. Hindwing below is dark cinnamon to chocolate brown with silver spots. Lacks heavy black scaling on veins. Wingspan 2 – 2 7/8″.

Similar Butterflies: Edwards' Fritillary has heavy black wing margins and lighter orange spots above matching its silver spots below. Edwards' and Callippe Fritillary have green disk below. Variegated Fritillary is tawny-orange with no silver spots. Most Northwestern Fritillaries have unsilvered spots below.

Habitat: Moist prairies, flower gardens and mountain meadows; plains, foothills and montane.

This magnificent large fritillary stops on its favorite gaillardia, pausing long enough for us to photograph the complimentary hues of the flower and butterfly.

Host Plants: Violets.

Life Cycle: Adults fly late May-September, nectaring on wild bergamot, thistles and rabbitbrushes. The female searches leaves of violets for a suitable place to lay eggs. Chrysalis is covered in dying leaves on the ground during winter.

Edwards' Fritillary   *Speyeria edwardsii*

Appearance: Dark orange above with black border on both wings and large pale orange spots on hindwings. Greenish below with elongate metallic silver spots. Female forewings flushed with pinkish-red near body. Wingspan 2 1/8 – 2 3/4″.

Similar Butterflies: Fritillaries look very similar unless you are fortunate enough to photograph one and compare it to several species at your desk. Smaller Callippe Fritillary shows greenish with silvered spots below and light marginal lines above. It flies at higher elevations. As Edwards' nectar with closed wings, their large silver spots below, including two in the shape of an ice cream cone, distinguish them from other fritillaries.

Habitat: Shortgrass prairies, open pine forests and canyons; plains, foothills and montane.

Edwards' Fritillaries are most common from 8,000-9,500 feet, but males roam widely onto the plains. Females often nectar on thistles and coneflowers.

Host Plants: Violets.

Life Cycle: Adults fly May-September producing one brood. Caterpillar feeds on leaves of violets, then caterpillar or chrysalis overwinters in the leaf litter.

Northwestern Fritillary   *Speyeria hesperis*

Appearance: Above red-orange to pale orange and darkened toward body. Hindwing with weak black margins. Red-brown to orange-brown basal disk below with unsilvered (rarely silvered) spots. Wingspan 2 – 2 1/4".

Similar Butterflies: Atlantis Fritillary, which is not common locally, has silvered spots below with dark brown disk near body. Aphrodite Fritillary is bright orange, large and shows silvered spots below.

Habitat: Moist meadows, gulches and cool slopes; foothills and montane.

Northwestern Fritillaries nectar on yellow sunflowers and mints. Look for them on three-foot-tall golden-glow blossoms along mountain streams.

Host Plants: Violets.

Life Cycle: Adults fly June-September producing one brood. Eggs are laid in or near young violet leaves. Caterpillar is almost solid black with black-tipped orange spines and brown lines in the middle of its back. Chrysalises and some caterpillars overwinter in the leaf litter.

Mormon Fritillary
Speyeria mormonia

Appearance: Wings are short with a somewhat rounded appearance. The hindwings, below, are pale brown to green. On the upper side, large spots near the margins of the wings are yellow or cream. Flies with rapid wing beats near the ground. Wingspan 1 5/8 – 2".

Similar Butterflies: Mormon Fritillaries look distinctly different from other fritillaries. Mormons are more common in the higher altitudes. Aphrodite Fritillary is much brighter orange and more common at lower elevations. Edwards' Fritillary has a black margin on the upper side of both wings.

Habitat: Wet meadows from 6,000 ft. to above; upper foothills to sub-alpine. Though uncommon in the prairie and lower foothills, they do occasionally offer a pleasant surprise.

Host Plants: Violets, especially marsh violet.

Life Cycle: Eggs are laid in leaf litter near violets or hidden under living foliage. Compound whitish spines adorn the caterpillar. The adult flies May- September.

Checkerspots and Crescents

Arachne Checkerspot

Poladryas arachne

Appearance: Below hindwing orange with white bands and a distinct row of black spots in the white median band. Orange rings with black bands on the abdomen. Above brownish-orange with narrow black lines and two-toned paler median orange band. Blue-gray eyes. Wingspan 1 1/8 – 1 1/2".

Similar Butterflies: Variable Checkerspot has a black or blackish-brown ground color and red to orange, yellowish or white spotting above. Below, the hindwing has rows of orange and yellow spots. Northern Checkerspot is more common. Below it is creamy or pale yellow (not white) alternating with red-orange or orange bands and it has yellow antennal knobs.

Habitat: Open grasslands and meadows; foothills and montane.

Males avidly hilltop and set up a territory. They perch on a low spot usually with wings open, pumping occasionally. Rapid fliers, males dart off in search of females, then return to their perch. Females are seen more frequently on slopes.

Host Plants: Penstemons.

Life Cycle: Adults emerge from two broods in lower elevations and fly May-June, then early August-September. In higher altitudes the flights occur in July.

Gorgone Checkerspot

Chlosyne gorgone

Appearance: Above, orange areas form continuous rows in brown background. Pale chevrons line the black margin of hindwing. Below, a lightning-shaped whitish zigzag line decorates the middle of the beige and orange hindwing. The zigzag line on the hindwings below is a helpful field mark. Wingspan 1 1/8 – 1 3/8".

Similar Butterflies: Pearl Crescent, Northern Crescent and Silvery Checkerspot are similar above, but have plain patterns below. Checkerspots and crescent butterflies are difficult to identify unless they are nectaring, and even then identification may depend on a good photograph and careful review in several field guides.

Habitat: Wet sand or mud, prairies, ridges, ditches, gulches and open drier slopes; foothills and montane.

Host Plants: Sunflowers.

Life Cycle: Adults fly May-July producing two broods. Eggs are laid in clusters producing dozens of caterpillars on a single sunflower leaf. Half-grown caterpillars overwinter.

Northern Checkerspot

Chlosyne palla

Appearance: Above red-orange with a light yellow median band and darker orange postmedian row of spots. Below has checkered pattern of creamy or buff-yellow and red-orange rows. Antennae orange. Wingspan 1 1/8 – 1 1/4″.

Similar Butterflies: Rockslide Checkerspot is found only in the alpine. Arachne Checkerspot has white median band with a black dot row below.

Habitat: Stream courses and associated moist flats and grassy slopes in a wide variety of habitats; foothills and montane.

This checkerspot glides low to the ground and speeds up when disturbed. Males puddle on wet sand or mud and patrol up and down wooded slopes or canyon bottoms.

Host Plants: Asters, rabbitbrushes, fleabane daisies, goldenrods and other sunflowers.

Life Cycle: Adults fly May-August producing one brood. Caterpillar has many black bristly spines and rows of small white dots and orange dashes on back. It overwinters half-grown. Green eggs are laid in large masses. Larvae are gregarious while feeding and enter diapause in tight groups, typically within curled dead leaves.

Rockslide Checkerspot *Chlosyne damoetas*

Appearance: Dull orange above and checkered with blurred brown and black, dusky at base of wings. Alternating bands of orange and dull white below with black wing veins. Wingspan 1 1/4 – 1 1/2".

Similar Butterflies: Northern Checkerspot does not fly in the alpine. Its wing fringes are checkered and males are red-orange above.

Habitat: Talus slopes; alpine.

Chasing this butterfly over the talus is not easy. Take a sandwich and wait until the sun shines, then this active checkerspot may settle on a boulder near you.

Host Plants: Fleabanes.

Life Cycle: One flight late June-August. Clustered eggs hatch in one week. Tiny black-headed caterpillars feed together and may require two or more years to mature.

Pallid Crescent
(Pale Crescent)

Phyciodes pallida

Appearance: Pale orange with irregular black marks and spots above. Forewing above has squares and a black patch in center of trailing margin, while hindwing is buff-yellow with whitish submarginal bands below. Wingspan 1 1/4 – 1 3/4".

Similar Butterflies: Mylitta Crescent has no submarginal white spot row on underside of hindwing and lacks tell-tale black patch along trailing edge of forewing below. Where they occur together, these two crescents are difficult to differentiate.

Habitat: Open wooded canyons, stream courses and gullies; foothills and montane.

Pallid Crescents inhabit the north-central Rockies and eastern Great Basin, whereas the more cosmopolitan Mylittas range west from the Continental Divide to the Pacific shore and south into Arizona and New Mexico.

Host Plants: Thistles.

Life Cycle: Adults fly April-July laying eggs in clusters on thistles. Ocher-colored caterpillar has brown back-stripe, brown side-bands and branching spines. Brown chrysalis overwinters.

Pearl Crescent

Phyciodes tharos

Appearance: Male has orange banded areas above with wide black wing margins. Below, orange forewing has black patches along margin and several cream-colored spots. Purple-brown patch at outer corner of hindwing encloses a light crescent. Wingspan 1 – 1 1/2″.

Similar Butterflies: Field Crescent lacks purple-brown patch on hindwing around crescent and shows three colors above. Northern Crescent has rich orange regular-shaped checkers above.

Habitat: Forest openings, moist meadows, fields, roadsides and streamsides; plains, foothills and montane.

Pearl Crescents fly low over grasses with alternating flaps and glides. Adults nectar on asters, fleabanes and thistles. The light crescent surrounded by purple-brown below reminds us of a lady wearing a brown velvet dress while displaying an exquisite pearl.

Host Plants: Asters.

Life Cycle: Adults fly April-July, producing one brood. Eggs are laid on leaves in clusters. Caterpillar overwinters.

Northern Crescent

Phyciodes cocyta

Appearance: Orange and black above with large open orange postmedian and submarginal areas lacking fine black lines. Wings below show open yellow-orange areas and a pale tan marginal crescent patch. Wingspan 1 – 1 1/4″.

Similar Butterflies: Pearl Crescents are smaller and usually have more black lines traversing the open orange areas above. Pearls often occur around prairie puddles and streams.

The Northern Checkerspot is similar to the Northern Crescent, especially the female. Checkerspots have black-lined scallops around the base of their wings and a crescent surrounded by a brownish patch below. The male checkerspot has a wide orange band on the forewing; the hindwing has a large field of orange.

Habitat: Aspen groves, meadows and woodland openings near streams; foothills and montane.

The Northern Crescent, which ranges into the far North, seems to tolerate cool habitats in the Rockies.

Host Plants: Asters with large stem-clasping leaves.

Life Cycle: Flies May-August producing one brood. Caterpillar is pinkish with pink-gray spines.

Field Crescent

Phyciodes pulchella

Appearance: Tricolored above with black-brown patches. Females show yellow-buff and orange patches. Forewing has cream-yellow bar across the cell and small black patches. Antennal knobs black-brown. Wingspan 1 – 1 1/2".

Similar Butterflies: This crescent shows three distinct colors above separating it from other crescents and checkerspots in the Front Range. In addition, other similar-looking crescents have orange antenna clubs.

Habitat: Open areas, intermittent waterways and glades near stream courses; plains, foothills and montane.

We're delighted to find these three-colored crescents because they're easier to identify than many other crescents. At times we find ourselves in meadows during the day of their group emergence, with a dozen or more flying around our ankles.

Host Plants: Tansy aster, aster species and fleabane daisies.

Life Cycle: Adults are widespread April-August. Females lay green eggs in clusters. Caterpillars feed communally then overwinter. Chrysalis is light mottled brown.

Commas, Tortoiseshells and Mourning Cloak

Satyr Comma

Polygonia satyrus

Appearance: Forewing golden orange above with jagged wing edges. Golden brown below with a median line dividing a two-toned brownish surface. A silvery comma shows in the central part of the hindwing. Wingspan 1 3/4 – 2 1/16".

Similar Butterflies: The Hoary Comma is grayer with a two-toned surface below and is more common in the foothills. The Green Comma has scalloped gray to brownish-gray markings below and is often associated with aspen groves.

Habitat: Valleys with cottonwoods and willows; foothills and montane.

Males perch along forest trails, chase off interlopers and pursue females. Males visit scat and mud; both sexes visit thistle blossoms, willows, lilacs, overripe fruit and sap flows.

Host Plants: Nettles and hops.

Life Cycle: Adults hibernate and usually fly mid-March to September. The caterpillar is whitish above with spines.

Green Comma   *Polygonia faunus*

Appearance: Jagged wing edges. Above, orange with dark borders, black central spots and yellowish submarginal spots on the hindwing. Many scalloped gray to brownish gray markings on the surface below, with outer half lighter and a silver 'comma' in center of hindwing. Wingspan 1 3/8 – 2".

Similar Butterflies: The Hoary Comma has no distinct yellowish spots in the margin of the hindwing.

Habitat: Streams, creeks and moist meadows; higher foothills and mountains.

Adult Green Commas visit Canada thistles and asters for nectar or dung (for moist substances); in early spring they feed on sap flows. These commas can be found from 8,000 to 10,000 ft. or lower in cool, moist aspen groves.

Host Plants: Aspen, willows and gooseberry.

Life Cycle: Adults fly mid-August into September. They may overwinter in the Front Range and appear as worn adults in May and June, when they reproduce. Adults live 9-10 months, an unusually long flight period. Caterpillars are yellow-brown to brick red with a white back. The spines are white.

Hoary Comma   *Polygonia gracilis*

Appearance: Two-toned, gray leaf-like appearance below, with jagged wing edges and silver comma mark on hindwing. Russet-orange above with diffuse yellow submarginal spotting on most posterior portion of hindwing. Wingspan 1 1/2 – 1 7/8".

Similar Butterflies: Green Comma has yellow fawn-like spots on trailing edge of hindwing above. Satyr Comma is brownish below and bright golden-orange above.

Habitat: Open conifer forests, meadows, urban areas and prairies; plains, foothills, montane and alpine.

A former common name, Zephyr Anglewing, poetically describes this comma's affinity for wind-caressed western meadows. The Hoary is common in early spring until fall, flying rather high over small streams, often with Mourning Cloaks, then pausing on sun-warmed wood or a rock surface.

Host Plants: Currants.

Life Cycle: Adults overwinter under bark or in tree cavities and emerge from hibernation in early spring to mate and lay eggs. Adults may emerge from hibernation as early as February, then the next generation flies well into the fall. New adults emerge in July and fly until October.

Milbert's Tortoiseshell

Aglais milberti
(*Nymphalis milberti*)

Appearance: Dark brown inner wings and margins above contrast with bright yellow-orange submargins. Evenly bicolor (black and dark brown) and leaf-like below. Wingspan 1 1/2 – 2".

Similar Butterflies: California Tortoiseshell is larger, more uniformly orange above and much lighter below.

Habitat: Streamsides, wet meadows, prairies, urban areas and tundra; plains, foothills, montane and alpine.

Though not abundant in our area, these butterflies can appear practically anywhere, from tundra ridgetops to suburban gardens to dry washes on the prairie. Males patrol hilltops in the foothills and mountains. Often flies with Satyr Comma.

Host Plants: Nettles.

Life Cycle: Adults overwinter and may emerge as early as late February. Females lay batches of eggs in April and May. Caterpillars by the dozens may remain on the nettle leaves, sometimes inside webbing. Fresh adults emerge in July.

California Tortoiseshell
Nymphalis californica

Appearance: Showy bright orange with a dark border and few large black spots on the forewing above. Below mottled brown. The orange catches one's eyes as this butterfly flits from one sugary source to another. Wingspan 1 3/4 – 2 1/8".

Similar Butterflies: Milbert's Tortoiseshell is smaller and has a sunrise arc of orange and yellow across all four wings.

Habitat: Ridge tops (males), open brushy areas and open woods; foothills.

They are often seen nectaring among holly-grape on a slope or sharing a broken-branch sap flow with Mourning Cloaks.

Host Plants: Wild plum, aspen, birches and willows.

Life Cycle: Often seen in early spring after emerging from hibernation. Up to 250 eggs are laid on upper and lower leaf surfaces of host plant. The velvety-black caterpillar has mostly black spines with small yellow protuberances at their bases. The butterflies disperse from warmer areas to the foothills. The single summer generation is on the wing from early July to August in the foothills. Adults often appear tattered in the summer because they emerge the previous fall.

Mourning Cloak

Nymphalis antiopa

Appearance: Named for their dark and somber appearance. Striking velvet-brown above with pale yellow wing margins. Brilliant blue spots often show on submargins. Dark brown and leaf-like below with whitish wing margins. Wingspan 2 5/8 – 3 3/8".

Similar Butterflies: Milbert's Tortoiseshell has fiery orange and yellow wing submargins and orange spots on the forewings above.

Habitat: Streamsides, open woodlands and urban parks; plains, foothills and montane.

Host Plants: Willows, birches, cottonwood, elms and hackberry.

Life Cycle: Mourning Cloaks are among a half-dozen local butterflies that hibernate as adults. They overwinter under loose bark or in leaf litter, and are often the first butterflies to emerge on sunny late-winter days in February or March. Females lay eggs in April and May. Fresh adults emerge in midsummer. These new adults estivate during hot weather, fly for a short time in fall, then enter hibernation.

Admirals, Buckeye, Ladies and Emperor

Red Admiral
Vanessa atalanta

Appearance: Brown above with orange-red stripe on forewings, white spots near forewing tips and a thick orange marginal band on hindwings. Mottled below with orange-red, blue and white bands on forewings. Wingspan 1 3/4 – 2 1/2".

Similar Butterflies: This admiral-striped *Vanessa* is darker and more strikingly marked above than Painted, American or West Coast Lady.

Habitat: Streamside glades, wet meadows and urban parks; plains and foothills.

Before flowers bloom in spring, adults take nectar from tree sap, sometimes utilizing networks of holes drilled by sapsuckers and other woodpeckers.

Host Plants: Nettle and false nettle.

Life Cycle: Overwinters as an adult in its southern range. They do not tolerate cold winters but disperse northward to Colorado in the spring. Red Admirals produce two broods along the Front Range with adults flying April-August.

Weidemeyer's Admiral   *Limenitis weidemeyerii*

Appearance: Black above with wide white submarginal band. Hindwing below marked with prominent white panel, row of red submarginal spots and gray-white marginal spots. Wingspan 2 – 3 1/2".

Similar Butterflies: Mourning Cloak sports yellowish wing margins.

Habitat: Gardens, streamsides and aspen groves; foothills and montane.

Look for this striking Rocky Mountain resident floating over foothill stream courses lined with willows. Territorial males fly out from streamside perches to intercept interloping swallowtails, commas, skippers and dragonflies.

Host Plants: Willows, quaking aspen, cottonwood, chokecherry and serviceberries.

Life Cycle: Hump-backed yellow-green or gray caterpillars overwinter in leaf shelters. Adults emerge in May and fly through September.

Common Buckeye

Junonia coenia

Appearance: Rich brown above with two striking blue eye spots rimmed with gold on forewing and two on hindwing, and whitish area across forewing cell. Two orange cell bars. Pale brown below with prominent white bar and multicolored eyespot on forewing. The prominent eyespots on both the forewings and hindwings may serve to scare away predators. Wingspan 2 – 2 1/2".

Similar Butterflies: Common and Small Wood-Nymphs have one or two eyespots on the forewing, but no orange.

Habitat: Grasslands, open fields and gardens; plains and foothills.

Every few years, large numbers of buckeyes appear in grasslands at the base of the Front Range foothills in September and October.

Host Plants: Plantains, monkey-flowers, toadflax and owl-clover.

Life Cycle: Buckeyes do not reproduce in Colorado but the adults typically disperse into eastern Colorado from the south and east during late summer and fall.

Painted Lady

Vanessa cardui

Appearance: Orange and black above with white spots on black wingtips and heavy black mark on the inner part of forewing. Hindwing above and below has row of four unconnected submarginal eyespots. Wingspan 1 7/8 – 2 1/2".

Similar Butterflies: American Lady has less black on the wings above and two large eyespots on the hindwings below. West Coast Lady has squared-off wingtips and an orange bar near the wingtips.

Habitat: Fields, open forests, prairies and gardens; plains, foothills and montane.

Researchers are still considering whether the northward flight of Painted Ladies in spring is a simple dispersal or a true migration during which some adults return south in the fall. Frequent school releases complicate this picture.

Host Plants: Thistles, mallows, legumes and many others.

Life Cycle: Adults disperse throughout North America from the Desert Southwest. Sometimes millions of Painted Ladies disperse through eastern Colorado. Adults in this state raise 1-3 broods, but no life stage survives our winters.

West Coast Lady

Vanessa annabella

Appearance: Rich orange and black above with squared-off forewing tip and large orange bar a third of the way in from the wing tip on the forward edge (this bar is white in the other two ladies). Row of small blue eyespots on hindwing. Below has marginal row of small blue eyespots on hindwing, in contrast with the larger eyespots of the other two ladies. Wingspan 1 3/4 – 2".

Similar Butterflies: Painted Lady has rounded wingtips. American Lady has two large eyespots on hindwing below.

Habitat: Gardens, meadows, vacant lots and urban parks; mostly plains.

Host Plants: Mallows and hollyhock.

Life Cycle: Females lay eggs singly on upper side of mallow leaves; caterpillars weave leaves into a silken nest and feed within. Adults hibernate, but not in Colorado. Most of the West Coast Ladies in Colorado have probably dispersed here from the Pacific Coast. Concentrations appear on rabbitbrush plants in September and October every few years.

American Lady

Vanessa virginiensis

Appearance: Orange and black above with white spots and short stripe near wing tip. A submarginal row of 4-5 indigo-blue hindwing spots and a small white dot in an orange spot on the forewing. Below two large eyes on an olive and white webby background with multicolored forewing tips. Wingspan 1 3/4 – 2 1/8".

Similar Butterflies: Painted Lady has more black on the wings and paler orange-salmon color above, and usually four spots on the hindwing below. West Coast Lady has squared-off forewing tips and an orange bar near the wingtips.

Habitat: Fields, meadows, open forests, urban parks and forest edges; plains and foothills.

We find these ladies nectaring on mints and sunflowers in foothills canyons in the summer and congregating on blooming rabbitbrush in the fall.

Host Plants: Pussytoes, pearly everlasting and cudweeds.

Life Cycle: Caterpillars live in a nest of leaves held together by silk. Most adults overwinter in southern regions, then disperse north in the spring. This strategy may enable them to expand their breeding range as the climate warms. Adults and other stages probably cannot survive Colorado winters.

Hackberry Emperor

Asterocampa celtis

Appearance: Wings are orange-brown above with one or two bold eyespots in forewing submargin. Dark wingtips are spotted with white. Mottled gray below with a row of submarginal eyespots on both wings. Wingspan 1 1/2 – 2 1/4".

Similar Butterflies: Painted Lady, West Coast Lady and American Lady are striking orange and black above and show some orange below.

Habitat: Canyons, riparian woodlands and open forests; plains and foothills.

Adults feed on sap, rotting fruit, dung and carrion. Males often rest upside down on tree trunks or perch on tall, sunny branches as they watch for females.

Host Plants: Hackberry.

Life Cycle: One to two flights from May through August. Eggs are laid in clusters, then the yellow-green caterpillars overwinter in groups snuggled into rolled-up leaves.

Ringlet and Wood-Nymphs

'Ochre' Common Ringlet *Coenonympha tullia ochracea*

Appearance: Ocher to tan above. Ocher to gray below, with a pale median band on the hindwing and a yellow-ringed, bluish eyespot on the tip of the forewing. Wingspan 1 – 1 3/8".

Similar Butterflies: Ridings' Satyr, which is uncommon in our area, is grayish tan above and below with pale oblong white spots on the forewings above. Crescents show multi-colored patterns above. Coppers are brighter colored.

Habitat: Prairies, meadows and forest openings; plains, foothills and montane.

The slow, bouncy flight of these ringlets as they flutter over and through host grasses separates them from other butterflies. While flying, they appear to have their wings closed half the time.

Host Plants: Grasses.

Life Cycle: In April-September, males flutter over sunny, grassy areas looking for females. Caterpillars overwinter in mats of dead grass.

Common Wood-Nymph
Cercyonis pegala
(Common (Large) Wood-Nymph)

Appearance: Brown with two large yellow-rimmed eyespots on forewing below and often a row of smaller bluish eyespots on the hindwing below. Some individuals have a pale yellow patch surrounding eyespots on forewing above and below. Female is cocoa colored, male dark chocolate. Wingspan 1 7/8 – 2 5/8".

Similar Butterflies: Small Wood-Nymph has single or unequal-sized eyespots on forewing and lacks conspicuous eyespots on hindwing below.

Habitat: Grasslands and streamside meadows; plains, foothills and montane.

When we see these lovely dark butterflies sailing through the drying grasses, we know that summer is turning toward fall. They are abundant in mixed-grass and tallgrass prairies at the base of the foothills.

Host Plants: Grasses.

Life Cycle: Adults emerge in midsummer. After hatching in late summer, the tiny yellow-green caterpillars overwinter.

Small Wood-Nymph
(Small (Dark) Wood-Nymph)

Cercyonis oetus

Appearance: Brown above and below with a single eyespot or two unequal-sized eyespots on forewing, with the smaller spot closer to the wing margin. Wingspan 1 1/4 – 1 3/4".

Similar Butterflies: Common Wood-Nymph has equal-sized eyespots on forewing and often a row of eyespots on hindwing below.

Habitat: Meadows and forest openings; plains, foothills and montane.

These smaller wood-nymphs zigzag low to the ground in mountain canyons, occasionally alighting on yellow composites, buckwheats or mammal scat.

Host Plants: Grasses.

Life Cycle: Adults fly July-September and produce one brood. Green caterpillars with dark green and white stripes overwinter shortly after hatching.

Alpines and Arctics

Magdalena Alpine

Erebia magdalena

Appearance: Blackish-brown and unmarked above and below. Some newly emerged individuals show a greenish sheen. Wingspan 1 3/4 – 2 1/4".

Similar Butterflies: Colorado Alpine has two eyespots on forewing above and below. The rare Yellow-dotted Theano Alpine has a yellowish submarginal band on forewing and hindwing.

Habitat: Rock slides, screes and ridges; alpine.

Since they live above tree line, these alpines may be particularly susceptible to global warming. As the tree line creeps higher, their available habitat become smaller. Seeing these acrobatic butterflies course over talus slopes throughout June and July is a memorable Colorado wildlife spectacle.

Host Plants: Grasses and possibly sedges.

Life Cycle: Eggs are laid on grasses, sedges or nearby rocks. Caterpillars overwinter by crawling low beside grass-covered boulders.

Common Alpine

Erebia epipsodea

Appearance: Brown to reddish-brown above and below with eyespots surrounded by orange patches on both wings. Wingspan 1 1/2 – 1 7/8".

Similar Butterflies: Colorado Alpine lacks eyespots on hindwing and prominent orange patches. Yellow-dotted Theano Alpine lacks eyespots. Both are smaller.

Habitat: Meadows and forest openings; foothills, montane and alpine.

Despite its name, this alpine also flies far below the alpine tundra. In foothill and mountain meadows, males flutter low to the ground searching for females. Males alight on wildflowers for just a few seconds, rarely lingering long enough to permit a close look.

Host Plants: Grasses and possibly sedges.

Life Cycle: Adults fly May-September, producing one brood. Females lay eggs singly on grasses. Third- and fourth-instar caterpillars overwinter.

Chryxus Arctic

Oeneis chryxus

Appearance: Light brown to orange-brown above with one or two eyespots on forewing. Striated brown and gray below, often with submarginal eyespots on forewing and hindwing. Prominent jagged mid-wing band. Wingspan 1 5/8 – 2 1/8".

Similar Butterflies: Uhler's Arctic is more silver-buff below and usually lacks the prominent jagged brown median line on the hindwing below.

Habitat: Open conifer forests and high ridges; foothills, montane and alpine.

Males select distinct territories and chase away other males.

Host Plants: Grasses and sedges.

Life Cycle: Adults fly May-August during even-numbered years in the Rockies; in odd-numbered years adults emerge in the Sierra Nevada. Young caterpillars overwinter, resume feeding the following summer, then hibernate again.

Uhler's Arctic   *Oeneis uhleri*

Appearance: Pale brown to orange-brown above with several submarginal eyespots on forewing and hindwing. Spots are sometimes reduced or nearly absent. Striated brown and silver-buff with some small submarginal eyespots below. Wingspan 1 1/2 – 1 7/8".

Similar Butterflies: Chryxus Arctic usually has a dark brown median line pointing outward on hindwing below and fewer and larger eyespots. Note slow and indirect flight of Uhler's Arctic as it flits through the grasses.

Habitat: Meadows, dry slopes and hilltops; foothills, montane and alpine.

Differences in flight patterns and habitats can help to separate our two common and similar-looking arctics. Uhler's sails and hovers over wildflowers or grassy slopes, whereas Chryxus tends to dart from perch to perch among conifers.

Host Plants: Grasses and sedges.

Life Cycle: Adults fly May-July producing one brood. Caterpillars hibernate then pupate the following spring.

Skippers

Silver-spotted Skipper

Epargyreus clarus

Appearance: Large with brown-black wings and translucent gold forewing bands above. Metallic silver band on hindwing below. Wingspan 1 5/8 – 1 7/8″.

Similar Butterflies: This conspicuous skipper resembles no other butterfly except for a few rare strays from Mexico.

Habitat: Stream edges in prairies, canyons, riparian forests, open woods, parks and gardens; plains and foothills.

This skipper, adapted to suburbs, occupies one of the most extensive ranges in North America. Males often circle upwards around each other, creating spectacular aerial displays.

Host Plants: Wild licorice, locusts and other legumes.

Life Cycle: Adults fly May-August producing one brood. Green, globular eggs hatch into caterpillars that are light green with darker green lines, patches and speckles. Caterpillars form a brown chrysalis that overwinters within a loose cocoon among ground litter.

Pacuvius Duskywing

Erynnis pacuvius

Appearance: Above, dusky brown-black with white trailing edges on plain brown hindwings. Orange-brown patch often shows in the middle of distinctly patterned forewing. Below, hindwing may show submarginal pale spots. Light rings encircle abdomen. Strikingly beautiful when newly emerged but difficult to identify when worn. Wingspan 1 1/8 – 1 1/2".

Similar Butterflies: Persius and Afranius Duskywings have no white fringe on trailing edge of hindwings and a less contrasting wing pattern above.

Habitat: Moist sand, streamsides and brushy slopes; foothills and montane.

Males perch on hilltops awaiting receptive females and use their hind leg brushes to fan or disperse their pheromones.

Host Plants: Buckbrush.

Life Cycle: Adults fly May-August and females lay green eggs that turn pink. Overwintering caterpillar is light green with black head showing orange patterning.

Persius Duskywing *Erynnis persius*

Appearance: Forewing above patterned with three small but conspicuous glassy dots toward wingtips. Look for gray forewing patch at end of cell and dark brown fringes on the hindwings. Wingspan 1 – 1 3/8″.

Similar Butterflies: Pacuvius Duskywing has whitish fringes on hindwing but is similar. It flies May-August. Afranius Duskywing has no clear spots on forewing and has a light brown spot on the mid-forewing.

Habitat: Meadows, streamsides, sandy flats and tundra; foothills, montane and low alpine.

This duskywing is fairly common in golden banner patches. In the tips of the new foliage, look for a rolled leaf, which if unrolled carefully could expose a Persius caterpillar.

Host Plants: Golden banner, milk vetches and other legumes.

Life Cycle: Adults fly May-July producing one brood. Green egg changes to pink before it hatches into a white-specked, hairy green caterpillar that overwinters.

Grizzled Skipper   *Pyrgus centaureae*

Appearance: Blackish-brown above with two bands of bright white spots across forewings. Pink wing fringes are checkered white and show black tufts at vein endings. Antennae pink. Wingspan 7/8 – 1 1/4".

Similar Butterflies: Two-banded Checkered Skipper has two white spot bands on its forewing forming an apparent "X". It lives at lower elevations among ponderosa pine, often in burned areas.

Habitat: Moist tundra and clearings in spruce forest; montane and alpine.

While visiting moist high mountain meadows and tundra in odd-numbered years you may see this small butterfly flashing black and white speckles around patches of green cinquefoil.

Host Plants: Cinquefoils.

Life Cycle: Adults fly in odd-numbered years producing one brood mainly June-July. Eggs are laid singly on herbs of the rose family.

Common Checkered-Skipper

Burnsius communis
(Pyrgus communis)

Appearance: Checkered black and white above. Males have blue-gray tone with bluish hairy scaling at base of wings. Females appear black with smaller areas of white checkering. Below, hindwing is gray-white to gray-brown with pale tan and olive bands of variable width. Fringes slightly checkered. Wingspan 7/8 – 1 1/4″.

Similar Butterflies: Small Checkered Skipper is tiny with white fringe incompletely checkered and is found on arid alkali flats. Grizzled and Two-Banded Checkered Skipper occupy high elevations.

Habitat: Weedy fields, roadsides, riverbanks, valley bottoms, vacant lots and parks; plains, foothills and sometimes montane.

This most common North American skipper looks bluish when flying. It is often identified by its habitat.

Host Plants: Mallows including hollyhock.

Life Cycle: Multiple broods produced April-September. Eggs change from green to cream-color and hatch into tan caterpillar. Chrysalis may not survive our winters, but adults fly north to the Front Range in spring.

Common Sootywing   *Pholisora catullus*

Appearance: Small, glossy black above with a curved row of a few small white spots on forewing and white spectacles on the head. Black below. Long, rounded wings. Wingspan 7/8 – 1″.

Similar Butterflies: Russet Skipperling is small, mostly unmarked dark brown above and rich red-brown below.

Habitat: Landfills, roadsides, agricultural areas, vacant lots and gardens; plains, foothills and sometimes montane.

This distinctive skipper thrives in a variety of habitats throughout North America and flies over weedy landscapes where butterflies are unexpected. It is the most widespread of small black skippers.

Host Plants: Lamb's quarters and amaranths.

Life Cycle: Adults fly April-September producing two broods. Caterpillar is pale green with straw-colored flecks and dark head. It makes shelter by bending leaves toward their midvein and fastening the edges with silk. Caterpillar overwinters in a stronger and larger tent. Chrysalis purple-brown.

Russet Skipperling

Piruna pirus

Appearance: Reddish-brown with small white spot pattern above and below. Wings are darker brown above. The body and wings are narrower than many butterflies. The flashing dark, light, dark, light of the Russet Skipperling's wings may help it escape a pursuing predator. It's a joyous event to see this tiny butterfly in the sunlight. Wingspan 7/8 – 1".

Similar Butterflies: Garita Skipperling has white wing fringes; Common Sootywing is glassy black with white spots on the forewing. Both of these have the same body shape as the Russet Skipperling but are smaller.

Habitat: Streamsides, moist meadows, irrigation canals; plains and foothills.

Host Plants: Wide-leaved grasses.

Life Cycle: Adults fly during June and July. Eggs are laid on the shaded underside of grasses. Larvae make an overnight protective nest by rolling the leaf from the tip. Late-stage caterpillars overwinter.

Juba Skipper   *Hesperia juba*

Appearance: Body thicker with shorter antennae than most butterflies. Forewing orange and brown with black margins extending between veins in inward jagged pointed margin. Hindwing below greenish or greenish-brown with orange along inner margin. White spots in band large and squarish. Wingspan 1 – 1 1/2".

Similar Butterflies: Many skippers look like the Juba Skipper, including the Common Branded Skipper and Pahaska Skipper, but those species may have wider and smoother dark wing margins. In general, skippers need to be photographed and identified "at the desk," because they are so similar and skip out of sight so quickly.

Habitat: Arid grassy brushlands and plateaus; foothills.

Host Plants: Grasses, especially blue grama and smooth brome.

Life Cycle: Adults fly in spring and in fall, producing two broods. Eggs are laid on grasses in the spring and fall. Spring laying females choose needle-and-thread grasses, while fall laying females choose a brome. Caterpillars are tan with black head showing streak on the face. A skipper forming in the summer will emerge, while the fall chrysalis likely overwinters. The Juba Skipper may be more common in the fall when smooth brome flourishes.

Western Branded Skipper   *Hesperia colorado*

Appearance: Hindwing olive to ocher to reddish brown ornamented with two white or yellow chevrons of joined spots opening toward body. Above, brown border blends into orange wings that may or may not show lighter spots. Wingspan 7/8 – 1 3/8″.

Similar Butterflies: Green Skipper is greenish below and found in canyon bottoms. Woodland Skipper has three noticeable dark bars on forewings above. Tawny-edged Skipper has orange above and no chevrons. Identifying skippers is challenging, and variation in wing coloration adds to the difficulty.

Habitat: Grassy areas in woodlands, brush, forest and tundra; foothills, montane and alpine.

We associate these skippers with blossoming gumweeds. They also nectar on asters, gayfeathers and thistles.

Host Plants: Grasses and sedges.

Life Cycle: Adults fly June-September producing one brood. Caterpillar is tan with dark brown head marked with broad tan areas. Eggs overwinter.

Green Skipper

Hesperia viridis

Appearance: Dusky orange above with broad, diffuse brown borders. Hindwing below is bright ocher-green when fresh, fading to olive-brown. Forewing blackish at base, greenish toward tip. A silver-white chevron made of five connected spots ornaments the hindwing below. Wingspan 1 – 1 3/8″.

Similar Butterflies: Difficult to separate from Pahaska Skipper and best identified by location within habitat. Pahaska flies on hillsides and hilltops as opposed to gullies. Posterior arm of Pahaska's chevron near the abdomen is straight or parallel to hindwing margin, while Green's is concave. Pahaska has scales of yellow in the stigma; who would think to look into the male Green's forewing stigma scales to find black felt?

Habitat: Canyons, ravines and gullies; foothills and montane.

Host Plants: Native grasses including blue grama.

Life Cycle: Adults fly late May-August, producing one brood. Caterpillar tan with dark brown head. While feeding, caterpillars live in clumps of tied-together leaves. Adults nectar on rabbitbrushes.

Woodland Skipper

Ochlodes sylvanoides

Appearance: Forewing above tawny orange with dark border projecting inward between the veins. Three dark dashes on forewings of female, but two on male, the inner one being an elongated black stigma. Hindwing below yellow-brown to purplish with postmedian squarish yellow-cream spots often merged as band. The forewing pattern above reminds some butterfly watchers of three logs on a fire. Wingspan 3/4 – 1 1/8″.

Similar Butterflies: Long Dash has wide dark margin on forewing above and its hindwing below displays a postmedian band of large pale spots. Tawny-edged Skipper has orange along leading edge of forewing.

Habitat: Ridges, forest edges, roadsides, gardens, lawns and streambanks; foothills.

This ubiquitous skipper adapts to natural and altered habitats and accepts nectar sources eschewed by most species.

Host Plants: Tall broad-leaved grasses.

Life Cycle: Adults fly June-September producing one brood. Gray-green egg turns white. First-stage caterpillar overwinters, fattens in the spring, then estivates through heat of summer until it pupates in late summer.

Taxiles Skipper

Poanes taxiles

Appearance: Male is yellow-orange above with narrow scalloped black border and female is dark orange-brown above with pale orange patches on hindwings. Forewing below yellow-orange with darkened base and outer margin. Hindwing of female is violet-brown with gray patch near outer margin and pale postmedian spot band. The female's hindwing below is amazingly beautiful with traces of violet and purple colors. Wingspan 1 3/8 – 1 5/8″.

Similar Butterflies: Woodland Skipper has two dark rectangular bars on upper forewing. Western Branded Skipper has distinct chevrons on the hindwing below.

Habitat: Forest openings along stream and river valleys; foothills.

Perching and nectaring males are hard to miss around white, pink and purple flowers.

Host Plants: Tall broad-leaved grasses.

Life Cycle: Adults fly June-September, producing one brood. Orange-tan caterpillar with several brown lateral lines and red-brown head lives on tall grasses.

Snow's Skipper

Paratrytone snowi

Appearance: Dark brown, male with large hourglass black patch above; patch is white in female. The hindwing below is red-brown, usually with postmedian band of discrete yellow spots. Hindwing fringe is whitish. Wingspan 1 1/16 – 1 1/8".

Similar Butterflies: Female Taxiles Skipper is dark orange above and has gray-lavender sheen below. Snow's Skipper is noticeably red-brown whereas other skippers are orangish, greenish or yellow-brownish.

Habitat: Stream courses, pine woodlands and meadows; foothills and montane.

Its range is restricted to pine dropseed meadows.

Host Plants: Grasses, especially pine dropseed.

Life Cycle: One brood of adults flies during late June into late August.

Dun Skipper

Euphyes vestris

Appearance: Small. Dusky brown above and virtually unmarked. Gray-black unmarked wings below. Female may have tiny translucent spots on forewing above. Note golden-orange color of face and top of thorax. Wingspan 1 – 1 1/8″.

Similar Butterflies: Russet Skipperling has dark head and thorax. Common Sootywing is black.

Habitat: Warm damp trails, moist areas near streams and marshes; foothills.

As we walk foothill trails we often find Dun Skippers resting on damp spots ahead of us. This drab skipper is small and easy to identify once learned. Its white-colored spectacles, front legs and lower thorax are a surprise once we move in for a closer look.

Host Plants: Sedges.

Life Cycle: Adults produce one brood and fly June-August. Pale green eggs become red on top before hatching. Shiny green caterpillar has an overlay of silver striations with a tricolored head and black collar. Third-stage caterpillar overwinters.

References

Print sources:

Bray, Richard. 1996-2004. Checklist and flight times of Rocky Mountain National Park on Lava Cliffs and Flattop Mountain. Unpublished reports. [Estes Park, CO]: Rocky Mountain National Park.

Brock, Jim P. and Kenn Kaufman. 2003. Butterflies of North America. Boston: Houghton Mifflin.

Chu, Janet. 2002-18. Various titles. Inventories of butterflies in Boulder County Open Space properties: Anne U. White Trail, Caribou Ranch, Heil Valley Ranch, Southeast Buffer and Walker Ranch. [Boulder]: Boulder County Parks and Open Space. www.bouldercounty.org/open-space/education/research/

Chu, Janet. 2018. Butterfly inventories in nine open space areas: four transects included. Boulder, CO: Boulder County Parks & Open Space Department. Also Ft. Collins: C. P. Gillette Museum of Arthropod Diversity, Colorado State University. (Lepidoptera of North America series; no. 12).

Fisher, Michael S. 2005-2017. The butterflies of Colorado. Ft. Collins: C.P. Gillette Museum of Arthropod Diversity, Colorado State University. (Lepidoptera of North America series; no 7, parts 1, 2, 3, 4, 5, 6).

Glassberg, Jeffrey. 2001. Butterflies through binoculars: the West. New York: Oxford University Press.

Jones, Stephen R. 2006-18. Monthly April-September butterfly surveys in Upper Gregory Canyon and Long Canyon, Boulder Mountain Parks. Unpublished research data. Available on request from Boulder County Nature Association: www.bcna.org.

Jones, Stephen R. 2014-18. July and August butterfly surveys at Sawhill Ponds Wildlife Preserve, South Boulder Creek State Natural Area and Dodd Reservoir. Unpublished research data. Available on request from Boulder County Nature Association: www.bcna.org.

Jones, Stephen R. and Ruth Carol Cushman. 2004. The North American prairie. Boston: Houghton Mifflin. (Peterson field guide series).

Nunes, Christian. 2007-2018. Incidental observations at various locations, particularly the Eldorado Mountain area. Colorado Butterflies Google group. https://groups.google.com/group/coloradobutterflies

Opler, Paul A. 1999. A field guide to western butterflies. 2nd ed. Boston: Houghton Mifflin. (Peterson field guide series).

Opler, Paul A. and Andrew D. Warren. 2004. Scientific names list for butterfly species of North America, north of Mexico. Ft. Collins: C.P. Gillette Museum of Arthropod Diversity, Colorado State University. (Lepidoptera of North America; no. 4).

Pelham, Jonathan P. 2018. A catalogue of the butterflies of the United States and Canada. Butterflies of America. [Dallas]: Butterflies of America Foundation. https://butterfliesofamerica.com/US-Can-Cat.htm

Pyle, Robert Michael. 1992. The Audubon Society field guide to North American butterflies. New York: Alfred A. Knopf.

Scott, James A. 1986. The butterflies of North America: a natural history and field guide. Stanford: Stanford University Press.

Weber, William A. and Ronald C. Wittmann. 2012. Colorado flora: eastern slope. 4th ed. Boulder: University Press of Colorado.

Websites:

Cook, Cathy, Donn Cook, and Joe Krieg. Colorado front range butterflies. 2019 [Boulder County]: Boulder County Nature Association. https://coloradofrontrangebutterflies.com.

Lotts, Kelly, Thomas Naberhaus, coordinators. 2018. Butterflies and moths of North America. Butterfly and Moth Information Network. https://www.butterfliesandmoths.org

North American Butterfly Association. 2019. Morristown, NJ: North American Butterfly Association. www.naba.org. Includes Checklist of North American butterflies occurring north of Mexico. Edition 2.3, December 2016. https://www.naba.org/pubs/enames2_3.html.

Warren, Andrew D., Kim Davis, Mike Strangeland, Jonathan P. Pelham, Nick V. Grishin. 2017. Butterflies of America. [Dallas]: Butterflies of America Foundation. www.butterfliesofamerica.com

Xerces Society for Invertebrate Conservation. 2019. Portland, OR: Xerces Society for Invertebrate Conservation. www.xerces.org

Glossary

(See also the butterfly schematic in the Introduction.)

Abdomen: The terminal (third) body segment of an adult insect.

Above: The top side of the wings as seen from above.

Alba form: Wings are mostly white.

Alpine: The Rocky Mountain life zone that lies above treeline and is dominated by tundra vegetation.

Band: An elongated surface or section with parallel or roughly parallel sides. Wider than a line.

Bar: A short, often dark, rectangular mark on the wings.

Base (of wing): The portion of the wing that is attached to the butterfly's thorax.

Basking: Resting in sunlight to warm flight muscles.

Below: The underside of the wing, often facing the ground.

Borders (of wings): Outer edges.

Brood: A generation of butterflies hatched from the eggs laid by females of the previous generation; members of a brood fly during the same general time period.

Cell: A large area of each wing, near the forward edge, that is entirely enclosed by veins.

Cell Spot: A spot within a wing cell.

Checkered or **Checkering**: A chessboard-like pattern of usually dark markings.

Chevron: V-shaped spot or band, usually white or silvery.

Chrysalis (plural: chrysalises): The hard case surrounding a butterfly pupa as it transforms from a caterpillar to an adult. See also cocoon.

Cocoon: The soft protective case of silk or similar fibrous material that moth larvae and some butterfly larvae spin. See also chrysalis.

Costa: The forward (anterior) edge of both the forewing and the hindwing.

Diapause: A period of inactivity and reduced physiological function induced by environmental factors; more commonly occurs in a caterpillar or chrysalis than in adults.

Diffuse: Not concentrated or localized.

Disk: The central portion of a butterfly wing touching the costal and trailing margins.

Dispersal: Moving outward from a single location. Differs from a migration in that individuals don't return to their point of origin.

Dorsal: The upper surface of the wings. In this guide we use the term "upper."

Estivate: To spend the summer or part of the summer in an inactive state.

Exoskeleton: The hard protective outer covering of an insect's body.

Eyespot: A scale pattern on a wing resembling an eye with a rim and pupil of contrasting colors. See also tail spot.

Flight (of adult butterflies): The time when a single generation of butterflies has emerged from chrysalises and is visible flying.

Foothills: The geographic area intermediate between the plains and the high mountains and dominated by open conifer woodlands, grasslands and shrublands.

Forewings: Forward wings.

Fringe: The extreme outer edge of the wing.

Hibernate: To enter a period of dormancy or torpor during extreme cold.

Hindwing: The rear (posterior) wing of each pair.

Host: The larval food plant. The female lays her eggs on this type of plant; after the caterpillars hatch, they eat these plants.

Inner margin: The edge of the wing closest to the butterfly's body.

Instar: The stage between each of the three or four molts during the growth of a caterpillar.

Larva: The eating and growth stage of butterflies, that is, the caterpillar. (Plural: larvae.)

Leading edge: The front part of the wing.

Marbling: Darker scales over yellow on a wing in a marble pattern.

Margin: Edge, as in wing margin.

Median: The middle part of the wing.

Migration: A seasonal moving back and forth between breeding and wintering areas.

Montane: The area of the high mountains below treeline and dominated by conifer forests and aspen.

Molt: The shedding of the exoskeleton by the caterpillar, which permits growth.

Open (bands or spots): Uninterrupted by veins or other lines.

Outer margin: The edge of the wings farthest from the butterfly's body.

Overwinter: Pass the winter (in a particular life stage or place).

Pheromones: Sex-attractant scent molecules produced by scent scales.

Postmedian: Between the outer margin of the wing and the middle of the wing.

Pupa: The transition stage during which a caterpillar transforms into an adult. (Plural: pupae.)

Pupate. Transform from caterpillar to chrysalis.

Scale: A small, flattened plate forming part of the wing surface.

Scintillation: Sparkling caused by reflective scales.

Spermatophore: A case or capsule containing a number of sperm.

Spot band: A band made up of multiple connected or nearly connected spots.

Stigma or **stigma scale**: A bold, sharply defined patch of scent scales on the forewings of many male skippers and hairstreaks.

Submargin: Just inside the outer margin of the wing.

Submedian: Occurring toward the body from the middle of the wing.

Taxonomic order: A systematic arrangement that considers genetic, anatomical and other characteristics to understand the interrelationship of living organisms. Taxonomic order attempts to place families in an evolutionary sequence, with older families leading the list. As advances in gene sequencing of butterflies reveal new data, scientific names and taxonomic order will inevitably shift in the future.

Thorax: The central portion of an insect's body to which legs and wings are attached.

Tail: Posterior extension on the hindwing.

Tail spot: Spot located on the hindwing near a tail, which could be an eyespot.

Talus: A formation of rock debris at the base of a cliff, usually the result of a rockslide.

Veins: Stiffened tubes that support the membranes of the wing, like kite struts.

Ventral: The lower side of the wings. This side is seen when a butterfly perches with its wings closed. In this guide we use the term "below."

Wingspan: The measurement of open forewings.

Appendix

Boulder County Flight Times

Butterfly flight times (months when adult butterflies can be seen) are a seasonal and cyclic natural phenomenon. With repeated monitoring, we can document patterns in when butterflies are visible. The following flight times are based on observations made within Boulder County. We are thus likely to encounter these butterfly species again during the indicated seasons in the Boulder County area. In addition, the table provides a rough indication of flight times in other Front Range counties. The observer should take into consideration their position within the Front Range; for example, spring observations in northern counties are likely to shift somewhat later, while southern county observations will probably shift earlier. Not all species described in this book are listed on this table. On the other hand, there are a number of species in this list that are not discussed in the book; although they were observed in Boulder County, they are not typical enough to be included in the 100 species accounts.

To compile the data we used numerous recorded observations that spanned over 20 years: butterfly surveys conducted from 2002-2018 in Boulder County and City of Boulder open space properties (Anne U. White, Caribou Ranch, Dodd Reservoir, Eldorado Mountain, upper Gregory Canyon, Heil Ranch, Long Canyon, Sawhill Ponds, South Boulder Creek, South Grasslands and Walker Ranch) and 1996-2004 surveys in Rocky Mountain National Park. (Bray 1996-2004; Chu 2002-2018; Jones 2006-2018; Jones 2014-2018; Nunes 2007-2018). Many of the properties where the observations were recorded are open to the public and welcome your enjoyment of the numerous butterfly species.

Boulder County Butterflies - Flight Times

	Mar	Apr	May	Jun	Jul	Aug	Sep
PARNASSIAN AND SWALLOWTAILS							
Rocky Mtn. Parnassian							
Black Swallowtail							
Anise Swallowtail							
Indra Swallowtail							
Western Tiger Swallowtail							
Pale Swallowtail							
Two-tailed Swallowtail							
WHITES AND ORANGETIP							
Pine White							
Checkered White							
Western White							
Spring White							
Cabbage White							
Margined White							
Large Marble							
Olympia Marble							
Julia Orangetip							
SULPHURS							
Clouded Sulphur							
Orange Sulphur							
Southern Dogface							
Queen Alexandra's Slphr							
Mead's Sulphur							
Cloudless Sulphur							
Mexican Yellow							
Sleepy Orange							
Lyside Sulphur							
Dainty Sulphur							

Legend: Alpine | Montane | Foothills | Plains

Boulder County Butterflies - Flight Times

Alpine	Montane	Foothills	Plains

	Mar	Apr	May	Jun	Jul	Aug	Sep
COPPERS, ELFINS AND HAIRSTREAKS							
Lustrous Copper					▓	▓	
Bronze Copper			▓	▓	▓	▓	▓
Ruddy Copper					█	█	
Blue Copper			▓	▓	█	█	
Purplish Copper					█	█	
Gray Copper				▓	▓		
Moss' Elfin		▓					
Hoary Elfin		▓	█				
Western Pine Elfin	█	▓	█	█			
Brown Elfin	█	▓	█	█			
Western Green Hairstreak		▓	█				
White-lined Green Hrstrk		▓	█				
Juniper Hairstreak			▓				
Thicket Hairstreak			█	▓	▓	▓	▓
Coral Hairstreak					▓		
Striped Hairstreak					█		
Hedgerow Hairstreak					█	█	
Behr's Hairstreak					▓		
Gray Hairstreak	▓	▓	▓	▓	▓	█	▓
BLUES							
Western Tailed-Blue				█	▓	█	
Marine Blue					▓	█	▓
Pygmy-Blue							▓
Shasta Blue					█	█	
Echo Azure		▓	█	▓			
Hops Azure			▓	▓	▓		
Arrowhead Blue				█	█		
Silvery Blue			▓	█	█		
Rocky Mtn. Dotted-Blue			▓	█	▓	█	

132

	Mar	Apr	May	Jun	Jul	Aug	Sep
Reakirt's Blue			▓	▓	▓	▓	▓
Melissa Blue		▓	▓	▓	▓	▓	
Greenish Blue			▓	▓	▓	▓	
Boisduval's Blue			▓	▓	▓	▓	
Lupine Blue				▓	▓	▓	
Arctic Blue			▓		▓	▓	

MONARCH AND VICEROY

	Mar	Apr	May	Jun	Jul	Aug	Sep
Monarch			▓		▓	▓	▓
Viceroy				▓	▓	▓	

METALMARK AND SNOUT

	Mar	Apr	May	Jun	Jul	Aug	Sep
Nais Metalmark				▓	▓		
American Snout				▓	▓		

FRITILLARIES

	Mar	Apr	May	Jun	Jul	Aug	Sep
Variegated Fritillary		▓	▓	▓	▓		
Aphrodite Fritillary				▓	▓	▓	
Edwards' Fritillary			▓	▓	▓	▓	
Coronis Fritillary			▓		▓	▓	
Callippe Fritillary				▓	▓	▓	
Northwestern Fritillary				▓	▓	▓	
Mormon Fritillary			▓	▓	▓	▓	

CHECKERSPOTS AND CRESCENTS

	Mar	Apr	May	Jun	Jul	Aug	Sep
Arachne Checkerspot				▓	▓		
Gorgone Checkerspot			▓		▓	▓	
Silvery Checkerspot				▓	▓	▓	
Northern Checkerspot			▓	▓	▓		
Rockslide Checkerspot							
Variable Checkerspot				▓	▓		
Pallid Crescent	▓			▓	▓		
Pearl Crescent				▓	▓		
Northern Crescent			▓	▓	▓		
Field Crescent		▓	▓	▓	▓	▓	

Boulder County Butterflies - Flight Times

Alpine	Montane	Foothills	Plains

	Mar	Apr	May	Jun	Jul	Aug	Sep

COMMAS, TORTOISESHELLS, MOURNING CLOAK

	Mar	Apr	May	Jun	Jul	Aug	Sep
Satyr Comma			▨				
Green Comma				▬	▬		
Hoary Comma	▨	▨	▬	▬	▬	▬	
Milbert's Tortoiseshell	▬				▬		
California Tortoiseshell		▨					
Mourning Cloak		▬	▨	▨	▨	▨	

ADMIRALS, BUCKEYE, LADIES, EMPEROR

	Mar	Apr	May	Jun	Jul	Aug	Sep
Red Admiral			▨	▬		▬	
Weidemeyer's Admiral			▨	▬	▬		
Common Buckeye						▨	
Painted Lady		▨	▨				
West Coast Lady					▨		
American Lady			▨	▬	▬		
Hackberry Emperor				▨			

RINGLET AND WOOD-NYMPHS

	Mar	Apr	May	Jun	Jul	Aug	Sep
Common Ringlet			▨	▨			
Common Wood-Nymph				▨	▬	▬	
Small Wood-Nymph				▬	▬		

ALPINES AND ARCTICS

	Mar	Apr	May	Jun	Jul	Aug	Sep
Magdalena Alpine					▨	▨	
Common Alpine					▬	▬	
Chryxus Arctic			▬	▬			
Uhler's Arctic			▨	▬			

SKIPPERS

	Mar	Apr	May	Jun	Jul	Aug	Sep
Silver-spotted Skipper				▨	▨		
Northern Cloudywing			▨	▬	▨		
Dreamy Duskywing			▬	▬			
Pacuvius Duskywing			▨	▬			
Afranius Duskywing		▨	▨				

	Mar	Apr	May	Jun	Jul	Aug	Sep
Persius Duskywing			■	■	■		
Grizzled Skipper					■	■	
Two-banded Chkrd-Skppr			■	■			
Comm Checkered-Skippr		■	■		■	■	■
Common Sootywing		■	■		■		
Russet Skipperling					■	■	
Least Skipper				■	■	■	
Garita Skipperling				■	■		
Uncas Skipper			■	■			
Juba Skipper			■	■			
Western Branded Skipper				■		■	■
Ottoe Skipper					■	■	
Leonard Skipper							■
Pahaska Skipper				■	■		
Green Skipper			■	■			
Nevada Skipper				■			
Peck's Skipper						■	■
Draco Skipper				■	■		
Tawny-edged Skipper			■	■	■	■	
Arogos Skipper				■	■		
Long Dash				■	■		
Woodland Skipper				■	■	■	
Taxiles Skipper				■	■	■	
Two-spotted Skipper					■		
Dun Skipper				■	■	■	
Dusted Skipper			■	■			

Index